Resumes That Pack a Punch!

Resumes That Pack a Punch!

Creating Beefy Bullets That Grab, Hook, and Wow
Hiring Managers into Calling You for an Interview

Robert T. Uda, MBA, MS, BS^2

iUniverse, Inc.
New York Lincoln Shanghai

Resumes That Pack a Punch!
Creating Beefy Bullets That Grab, Hook,
and Wow Hiring Managers into Calling You for an Interview

Copyright © 2006 by Robert T. Uda

iUniverse books may be ordered through booksellers or by contacting:

iUniverse
2021 Pine Lake Road, Suite 100
Lincoln, NE 68512
www.iuniverse.com
1-800-Authors (1-800-288-4677)

ISBN-13: 978-0-595-38344-3 (pbk)
ISBN-13: 978-0-595-82717-6 (ebk)
ISBN-10: 0-595-38344-0 (pbk)
ISBN-10: 0-595-82717-9 (ebk)

Printed in the United States of America

Resumes That Pack a Punch! is dedicated to Dr. Regina J. Eisenbach, associate dean, College of Business Administration (CoBA), California State University, San Marcos (CSUSM). Dr. Eisenbach received her Ph.D. degree in Organizational Behavior from the University of Miami. She is an inspirational leader, administrator, and educator.

Contents

Preface

This book is about preparing powerful resumes and cover letters that pack a punch. It includes principles, strategies, and tactics for writing winning resumes, cover letters, and bullets that grab attention, hook the reader, and wow hiring managers into calling you for an interview. *Resumes That Pack a Punch! Creating Beefy Bullets That Grab, Hook, and Wow Hiring Managers into Calling You for an Interview* will open eyes, cause outside-of-the-box thinking, and promulgate paradigm shifts.

Resumes That Pack a Punch! works hand-in-hand with three other previous books I wrote and published. They are as follows:

- *Career Quest for College Graduates: Developing a Successful Career by Leveraging Each of Your Jobs*
- *Career Quest for College Students: Career Development for Those Who Plan to Have a Successful Career*
- *What Hue Is Your Bungee Cord? Job Searching Strategies for Those Over 40 Years of Age*

If you learn, internalize, and apply all of the principles enclosed in this book, you will be well on your way to preparing resumes and cover letters that will surely generate calls for interviews.

If you disagree with anything that I have written in this book, I encourage you to write me and voice your disagreement. I always like to hear and learn about other people's views on whatever I write. Never do I believe that I know all truth on anything. I am always willing to change my views if someone comes up with contrary responses that make sense to me. That being said, I look forward to hearing from you.

All writings and opinions in this book are solely mine. Any error would be my error only. If you find errors, please bring them to my attention. We will correct them in subsequent editions of this book. I hope you enjoy the real-life stories in this book as I thoroughly have enjoyed living and writing about them. Thank you.

Robert T. Uda
San Marcos, California
March 2006

Chapter 1   Resumes That Pack a Punch

In today's economy, you need to carefully present your experience to avoid being seen as unstable. Start by evaluating your situation and determining how bad it really is. If you are panicking about two months of unemployment back in 1984, your job search will probably not be affected. However, if you are dealing with recent periods of unemployment extending for months or even years, you will need to start strategizing.[1]

Kim Isaacs
Monster Resume Expert

This book is about preparing winning resumes and cover letters that pack a punch. Much of the material in this book resulted from answering student questions from courses on Career Development, which I had taught in the spring 2004, fall 2004, spring 2005, and fall 2005 semesters at the California State University at San Marcos (CSUSM).

Developing Your Resume

Developing your resume is a career-long process. You must continually work at it. I have iterated my resume hundreds of times—even over a thousand times—throughout the past 40 years of my career. With every job you have, think about what you can and must do to write in your resume superb accomplishments, achievements, performance, and results.

An "accomplishment" comprises a set of "achievements." For example, graduating with a bachelor of science in business administration (BSBA) and receiving

---

[1]   Kim Isaacs, "Spotty Work History Resume Tips: How to Handle Employment Gaps and Job-Hopping," Monster Resume Expert, http://flipdognews.monster.com/.

a degree diploma is an accomplishment. An achievement is successfully passing a course that is a component of the BSBA degree requirements. Successfully passing all required courses for the BSBA degree comprise the set of achievements.

I have developed resume-writing ideas and secrets throughout my career while conducting over a dozen major job searches. *Your resume is your entire career on an 8-1/2"x11" piece of paper.* So, spend the necessary time to make it a masterpiece.

If you find it difficult developing significant accomplishments for your previous jobs, then you must plan to accomplish significant projects on all future jobs from hereon out. If you do not plan your career, you will have nothing but jobs that show only position descriptions, responsibilities, and duties to include in your resume.

> *Your resume is your entire career on an 8-1/2"x11" piece of paper.*

You must be an employee who "makes a difference," "adds value," and is a "mover and shaker" in the company. If you do these things, you will receive awards, rewards, raises, promotions, bonuses, perquisites, and recognition/praises. These benefits represent the outward manifestations or evidences of your accomplishments, achievements, performance, and results.

Create Several Resumes

You should make at least two different resumes...one for your primary area of expertise and the other for your secondary area of expertise. Furthermore, if you have other areas of strength, you could develop third and fourth alternatives. Myself, I have about 10 different resumes (e.g., proposal development, business development, project/program management, counterterrorism, career counseling, consulting, teaching, engineering support services, technical writing, and telecommunications).

Dynamite Resume and Cover Letter

Prepare and polish your resume and cover letter continually so that they attract people, cause them to read entirely through them, and motivate hiring managers to call you for interviews. Create "beefy" bullets that "pack a punch," "grab" attention, "hook" the reader, and "wow" the hiring manager to call you in for an interview. Create bullets that accentuate your performance, results, accomplishments, and achievements. Create bullets that are quantitative, measurable, specific, factual, believable, meaningful, real, and time-phased. Create bullets with features and benefits. Avoid bullets that cover only job descriptions, responsibilities, and duties. If you cannot create good bullets on all of your past jobs, then make it a point to work hard and do significant things on all future jobs so that you will be able to write good bullets on future resume updates.

Good Resume Writing

I get a big kick out of the people who argue with me regarding different redlines (and sometimes conflicting) that they receive on their resumes from their career coach, their instructor, and the career center. *Good resume writing is an art, not a science.* As in science and math, resume writing is not "one plus one equals two." It is whatever that can be done to make the resume "sell you" and generate calls for interviews. That is it!

> *Good resume writing is an art, not a science.*

Take Full Responsibility for Your Resume

Remember this: As a career coach, I cannot and will not make any decision for you. I can only give you some of my thoughts, suggestions, experience, and knowledge. You must take all of that information, weigh the facts, and make the decision based on what you know, agree with, and feel what is right. You should take full responsibility for your decision no matter how things turn out.

Redline Changes

There are many different ways to prepare a good resume. This is why I tell job seekers to take only whatever redlines they totally and unequivocally agree with and incorporate those changes. If they feel a little doubtful, if they disagree by the slightest amount, and if they do not feel it is right, then they *should not* make the redline change.

Take Ownership

All job seekers should take ownership of whatever redline changes they accept and make. They should take full responsibility for their own resume. If things do not work out, they should not blame someone else for their poor choices. It should be likewise on both the interviewing process and the salary negotiating process.

Accept Responsibility

People these days do not like to take responsibility. They do not want to make choices. They do not want to take the blame for anything. They always want to blame their misfortunes on others. Remember, someone once said, "*Whenever you point a finger at another, you have three fingers pointing right back at yourself.*" So, whatever choice you or anyone else makes, stick with it whether the choice has positive results or negative consequences.

> *Whenever you point a finger at another, you have three fingers pointing right back at yourself.*

Apply Concepts and Principles

Remember these principles. They will guide you on a straight and narrow path throughout your life. I harp continuously for students and clients to learn, remember, and apply *concepts* and *principles*. If all students and clients would do that, they would do well in their careers and in life. That is what I call concept-based and principle-based leadership.

Examples of Good Resumes

Danielle Birdsall, one of my outstanding students, prepared an example of an excellent resume shown below. Note her "bullets that pack a punch." Then, on the subsequent page, we see another good resume example written by Michael Turner, another student in one of my classes.

DANIELLE L. BIRDSALL

1972 GLORIA STREET
SAN MARCOS, CA 92078

PHONE 760 752-2960 • CELL 760 752-5355 • BIRDS999@CSUSM.EDU

OBJECTIVE

To secure a position in a dynamic, challenging, and growth oriented company that will allow me to apply my proficient management and marketing skills.

SUMMARY

Accomplished communicator. Team oriented. Highly competitive with a disciplined mind set towards successful execution. Extremely confident with effective interpersonal skills and unquestioned integrity.

EDUCATION

Bachelor of Science in Business Administration (BSBA), May 2005
1. Option in: Service Sector Management (SSM)
2. Deans List 4 Semesters
- Grade Point Average: 3.44
- California State University San Marcos (CSUSM)

EXPERIENCE

Consultant — 2004 – present
Senior Experience, CSUSM, San Marcos, CA
- Serves on a five-member team to research new approaches of implementing gratuities to make the "tipping" operations more competent for both technicians and guests for the Golden Door Spa.
- Awarded an "A" grade on the completed semester of the Senior Experience project.

Soccer Coach, Seasonal — 2001 – present
British Academy of Soccer Sciences, La Mesa, CA.
- Single -coaches 8 to 15 children ages 7 to 13 each session allowing for the club to cut costs to $10 per session and raise demand by approximately 20 percent.
- Motivates youth and helps them develop their individual strengths through soccer drills and instruction.

Receptionist — 2002 – 2005
Joelle's Hair Salon and Day Spa, San Diego, CA
- Received four consecutive raises within my two+ years of employment.
- Accredited with scores of 90 out of 100 and above during biannual reviews for outstanding performance.
- Administrated salon operations without supervision, conducted Joelle's opening operations single-handedly, and assisted in training of new hires.

Youth Leader — 2003 – 2004
Rancho YMCA, San Diego, CA
Worked with children ages 10 through 14 to help them develop intellectually and socially with their peers.
- Organized training and team building exercises winning 4 of our 5 competitions over the season.
- Attended nine training sessions and received recognition as being the outstanding novice.

Athletic Coach — 2001– 2002
Special Olympics, San Diego, CA
- Assisted in their mental and physical development through a variety of track and field sports.
- Worked with approximately 50 special needs children of various ages increasing hands-on training by 25 percent.

SKILLS

- One year of American Sign Language.
- Four years of Spanish.
- Exceptional communication skills.
- Knowledgeable in computer programs such as: Microsoft Word, Microsoft Excel, Windows XP, Windows 98, Windows 2000, Microsoft Office, Microsoft Access, PowerPoint, Adobe Photoshop, Adobe Acrobat, and Internet.
- First-Aid certified.

AWARDS RECEIVED

Sundevil Standout, 1998, 1999, 2000, High School Student Acknowledgment Award
Most Inspirational Player, 1999 High School Soccer
Most Athletic, 1997 School Award

Note that there is no standard, universal, best way to prepare a good resume. The bottom line to good resume writing is that if your resume generates calls for scheduling interviews with you, then it is a good resume. Your resume has sold you to the hiring manager to motivate him/her to schedule you for an interview.

Michael William Turner

1077 Treadwell Avenue - Simi Valley, CA 93065-5039 - 619.925.9039 - turntek@hotmail.com

SUMMARY QUALIFICATIONS

Cross-functional, results-driven professional with unique ability to handle multiple tasks *en route* to achieving company goals and objectives. Strong interpersonal supervisory, communication, and organizational skills. Displays relationship-building and problem-solving skills resulting in high productivity while demonstrating proficiency in meeting objectives in a timely manner. Expertise in MS Excel, Word, PowerPoint, Outlook, HTML, and IBM AS/400.

EDUCATION

California State University San Marcos   San Marcos, CA   May 2004
Bachelor of Science in Business Administration, Finance Emphasis
Dean's Honor Roll, 2 Semesters, GPA 3.51

PROFESSIONAL EXPERIENCE

California State University San Marcos   San Marcos, CA   2003 – Present
Consultant, Senior Experience Project

- Moderated an Economic Summit with the 14 communities in San Diego North County to discover the strengths, challenges, opportunities, and threats that concern the County.
- Developing a marketing plan to attract and retain the *Creative Class* target market to be implemented by San Diego North Economic Development Council in May 2004.

Tequila Los Abuelos, S.A. de C.V.   Tequila, Jalisco, Mexico   2003 – Present
Independent Consultant

- Prepared market and industry analysis of potential markets including market size, competitors, industry trends, and other key data to assist sales representatives generate $511,000 in new accounts in the United States and Mexico.
- Researched and recommended a label designer artist to complete labels for the new venture that saved the owner $20,000 in labeling costs.

Costco Wholesale   Northridge, La Mesa, and Mission Valley, CA   1995 – 2001
Return-to-Vendor Clerk

- Promoted from *Sales Associate* to *Return-to-Vendor Clerk* with hourly rate change from $15.00 to $16.67 per hour (an 11.13 percent increase) for excellent performance.
- Consistently reduced losses by beating projected shrink levels to a .85 percent level relative to semiannual profits, which resulted in a $1,423.00 bonus.

Frank Black Tours   Los Angeles, CA   1996 – 1997
Stage and Guitar Technician

Chapter 2   Beefy Bullets That Grab, Hook, and Wow

'When we do a keyword search, sometimes we just look at job titles. Tweak your job title to reflect your actual duties and what is common to the rest of the world,' said recruiter Khris Klimowicz of Milwaukee, Wisconsin. When asked for an example, she said, 'Paraprofessional.' I said, 'That's like a teacher's aid.' She said, 'Why not so? Everyone knows what a teacher's aid is.'

Other tips she recommends:

1) Use a professional email address. No goofy names. No birth dates in the address. First initial, last name is the recommendation

2) Review your employment dates to see if they are logical. Did you really start work in 1896 or was that a typo?

3) Use normal, common sense language, not corporate jargon or odd titles. 'Clerk, Level 2' has no specific identity in the real world.[2]

Wendy Terwelp, Career Coach

Resumes That Pack a Punch

Accentuate Achievements, Accomplishments, Performance, and Results

The biggest problem I see with most resumes is that they do not have bulleted items under each job that "pack a punch" and "hook" the reader. Most resumes include bullets that are nothing but job descriptions, duties, and responsibilities. To pack a punch, these bullets must be achievements, accomplishments,

---

2   Wendy Terwelp, Career Coach, "Quick Tips for Better Resume Response," *The Career News*, Vol. 5, Issue 3, January 17, 2005.

performance, and results. They should be significant, measurable, quantitative, and pack the "Wow!" factor. They should include both a feature and a benefit.

Be a Standout Employee

You must be an employee who "makes a difference," "adds value," and is a "mover and shaker" in the company. If you do these things, you will receive awards, rewards, raises, promotions, bonuses, perks, and recognition/praises. These will be the outward manifestations or evidences of your accomplishments, achievements, performance, and results. I hope you see what I am driving at here.

Bullets That Pack a Punch

I am in my current job because I was recruited while working for another company. My current boss came into my work, liked what he saw, and offered me a job on the spot. Should I include this as a bullet on my resume, and if so, do you have ideas on how to pack a punch with that?—Leah Belmonte

Yes and no. Yes, you can create and use a bullet to describe your previous job. No, you should not use this bullet to describe your new job. Since I do not know what you have done on your previous job, I do not know how to create the "feature" for your bullet; however, the "benefit" to this bullet can be the fact that you were "offered a job on the spot." Hence, if, for example, you were the top producer in the company on your previous job, say bringing in revenues of $5,000 a day, then, you can write the bullet as such:

- Sold on average $5,000 of goods per day, impressed a visiting hiring manager, and received a job offer on the spot.

Because I do not know the background of your previous job, I made up the $5,000 of goods per day just to create a "feature" to your bullet. You would need to insert the real facts that motivated your new boss to make you such an offer "on the spot."

Examples of Good Resume Bullets

To give you a better idea of what I mean here, I have listed below some bullets from my resume to show you similar significant achievements, unique accomplishments, superior performance, and memorable results that I want to see you likewise develop:

- Assisted in winning a $22M contract with projected future revenues of $300M to $500M.
- Contributed significantly to winning $80.5M of new business and achieved a win ratio of over 85 percent.
- Rewarded with over $20K of bonuses for results in winning $80M of new business.
- Honored with corporate award for outstanding performance as Marketing Performer of the Year 2000.
- Contributed to winning 20 contracts with total value of around $650M of bookings.
- Conceptualized and championed the Proposal Development System (PDS) that transformed a win ratio from 8 percent to 65 percent over two years.
- Received $11K in performance bonus and about $840K of stock-option incentive income for successes.
- Captured 14 of 17 software services contracts for a total value of $15M.
- Achieved an 82 percent win ratio and received $35K bonus for successes.
- Contributed significantly to winning a $52M contract on the Land Warrior (LW) proposal.
- Assisted in winning a $30M contract on the CORPS Surface-to-Air Missile (SAM) proposal.
- Won over 75 percent of all proposals comprising over $200M of new business.
- Captured over 50 percent of all competitive proposals for over $200M of new business.

Resumes That Generate Calls for Interviews

Do you get the idea of what I mean by significant accomplishments, achievements, performance, and results that are quantitative and measurable, pack a punch, and hook the reader with the "Wow!" factor? This is what you should do for your resume. If you will do that, you will receive many calls for interviews.

Developing the "Wow" in Your Resume

Seek Project Work to Perform

At times, one cannot generate good bullets from the jobs previously held because they were just mundane jobs. However, you can obtain better, future jobs. What that should indicate to you is that you should look for good, meaningful jobs through which you can perform and accomplish significant things (i.e., measurable projects) instead of just pushing a pencil, shuffling papers, filing papers, sweeping the floor, getting the coffee, and washing the dishes. That is why a good education is very important!

Add Value to Your Resume

Additionally, good networking will help you acquire the "connections" you need to "get a break" and receive good offers instead of just manual positions doing menial labor. Furthermore, I encourage you to get involved in extracurricular activities that can bolster your resume with significant offices held, membership in honorary organizations, awards won, and other such pluses that can raise the "value" of your resume and your stature among your peers.

Ideas for Bolstering Your Resume

You can also do some of the following things to bolster your resume:

- Earn advanced degrees
- Learn foreign languages
- Join and participate in professional organizations
- Work hard in your jobs so that you get "something of value" for your work, e.g.,
  - Bonuses
  - Raises
  - Promotions
  - Recognition
    - Awards, e.g., savings bonds, certificates, plaques, and gift certificates
    - Rewards (money)
    - Praises, pats on the back, strokes, warm fuzzies, compliments in the presence of others, and verbal thanks

- ○ Perquisites (Perks)
- ○ Meaningful Correspondence
  - ▪ Letters of Appreciation
  - ▪ Thank you letters and emails
  - ▪ Letters of Congratulations
  - ▪ Letters of Recommendation
- Write technical papers
  - ○ Present them at conferences
  - ○ Publish them in journals
- Write/publish books and other publications
- Discover things
- Invent things and obtain patents on your inventions
- Create/innovate things, e.g., systems, projects, programs, and events
- Get on "Blue Ribbon" Committees and "Tiger" Teams
- Work on proposals
- Attend conferences, seminars, workshops, trade shows, and meetings
- Work for and earn "sought-after" certifications
- Join clubs and organizations, run for offices, and serve in those clubs and organizations
- Apply for awards and recognitions such as "Who's Who" publications when you've built up a good record
- Take free computer courses at career centers and hone your computer skills

Build an Extensive Curriculum Vita and/or Dossier

You can be involved in and do hundreds of other activities to enhance your resume and your stature in your chosen industry. Do you get the picture of what I am driving at here? Yes, if you have accomplished nothing of significance, you cannot write bullets that grab people's attention and "Wow" them. So, start working right now to build an extensive curriculum vita and/or dossier. Remember, today is the first day of the rest of your career and life.

More "Wow" for the Resume

A Mere Summer Job

I worked on a summer job for three months as a "gas pump jockey" (a menial job indeed) at a gas station in Hawaii over 40 years ago back in the early 1960s. In those caveman days, it was called "service stations," where we really "serviced" the cars coming into the station instead of just filling it with gas.

Make a Mark

For example, besides filling the tank with gas, I cleaned all of the windows, filled the radiator with water, checked the oil level, and, if oil was required, poured a quart of oil into the crankcase, and checked the tire pressure of all tires. I worked very hard and made the customers happy.

Differentiate Yourself

I ran whenever I needed to get from point A to point B. I did more than just "service" the cars. I changed and patched tires, lubed cars, washed and polished cars, changed the oil and oil filters, and filled hydraulic oil in the braking system. Those tasks were not even part of my job description!

Receiving a Bonus

The service station owner was so impressed with me that, on my last working day before returning to the University of Oklahoma, he took a $20 bill out of his cash register and handed it to me as a going-away bonus. Now, let me tell you, over 43 years ago that $20 then, taking into consideration the inflation rate over 43 years, would be well over $150 today. One could calculate using a time-value-of-money accounting formula exactly what the $20 in 1963 dollars would be valued at in today's (2006) dollars.

Generating a Good Resume Bullet

I held that job when I was still in college. So, if I were to write my resume of that time, do you not think I could have written a good bullet about that job? That bullet would cover the fact that I did all those good things for the customers, which made them very happy. Then, the job ultimately ended with my receiving a good $20 bonus from my boss, the owner of the service station. Do you think that story could make a good "Wow!" bullet on my resume of that day? To wit,

- *Serviced cars in such a manner that achieved 100 percent satisfied customers. As a result, received a $20 bonus from the service station owner on the last day of work in recognition of value-added contribution to his business.*

Who Said You Cannot Make Good Bullets With Menial Jobs?

See, if you can show a positive result of your happy customers (both internal and external), that approach makes your bullet a "Wow!" Remember, over 43 years ago, $20 then is worth over $150 today. Thus, for just a three-month summer job, receiving $150 today would be a nice bonus indeed! Remember, it was just for working in a service station as a gas pump jockey!

You may not be able to make performing administrative duties measurable like I did with examples of the bullets that I had shown earlier of my previous jobs. However, you can add some measurability to it as I did in the service station bullet above.

The "Wow" Outcome

The "Wow!" outcome is the bonus received. So, if you received any kind of promotion, bonus, raise, award, and recognition in any form such as a thank you letter, certificate, or praise, that could be added to your bullet to give it some "punch." Do you see what I am saying here?

A "Wow" Resume of a High School Graduate

I dug up a two-year old resume of my 22-year old daughter (Heather) at the time (she is now 26). She is only a high school graduate with no college degree. She worked for Washington Mutual Bank for four years from 18-22 years of age… starting right out of high school.

Example of a High School Graduate's Resume

This is what she had on her resume after four years of work there:

WASHINGTON MUTUAL BANK, Vista & San Marcos, CA

1998-2002

Senior Personal Financial Representative, Personal Financial Representative, Senior Teller, and *Teller*

Performed new accounts and customer service while managing and performing the origination, processing, and funding of consumer and residential loan pipelines.

- Promoted from *Teller* to *Senior Teller* with hourly rate change from $8.00 to $10.00 per hour (a 25 percent increase) for excellent performance.

- Promoted from *Senior Teller* to *Personal Financial Representative* with salary change to receive incentive ($10.00 per hour plus average $500 monthly incentive) for excelling in teller responsibilities and completing New Account Training.

- Promoted from *Personal Financial Representative* to *Senior Personal Financial Representative* with salary change to receive higher incentive ($1,700 per month plus average $2,100 monthly incentive) for meeting goals in consumer lending and completing *Residential Loan Training.*

- Funded (as an individual) approximately $500 thousand in consumer loans per month and approximately $800 thousand in residential loans per month.

- Assisted in funding (as a branch) approximately $1 million in consumer loans per month and approximately $2 million in residential loans per month.

- Presented with the *Branch Quarterly MVP Award* in 1998, 1999, and 2000.

- Scored 100 percent perfect shop scores through *Secret Shopper Program* 9-out-of-10 times. The 10th time was scored at 98 percent.

- Received the *Crime Stopper Award* in 2001 for preventing a crime in the bank.

Leveraging to Advance Your Position

She had received a promotion each year, recognition, awards, and advanced training. She used that job to get into her next job making over $50K per year managing a 96-unit apartment complex. She was also hired as the cheerleading coach of the new high school in San Marcos, California. Obviously, she has leveraged her significant accomplishments, achievements, performance, and results to advance her position.

Applying a Well-Leveraged Background

She has again recently leveraged her apartment complex management position, which she held for three years, into another loaning representative position back with Washington Mutual that could earn her up to $100K per year. Soon she will be making more money than I am making! I am now trying to encourage her to go get a college degree to give her income some credibility.

It Can Be Done

This indicates that even a high school graduate can develop a "Wow!" resume by achieving the kind of accomplishments that put a punch in her resume. Further, she developed her resume all by herself without any help from Dad. All she did was to look at my resume, and then she acquired the necessary ideas to prepare her own winning resume. It can be done.

A Resume With "Hooks" That "Grab" and "Pack a Punch"

A Recent College Graduate's Resume

To give you another idea of what can be done to develop a resume that has "hooks" and "packs a punch," I have attached an excerpt of my son's (Marc) resume, which he developed from jobs and schooling over the past five years. I sanitized the resume by deleting the header, contact information, and other personal information. He is 29 years old.

Build a Planned Resume

Note that you can plan your career (even from the beginning) by obtaining jobs that are good, solid jobs. Work on obtaining them in a sequence such that later jobs build upon earlier jobs. In other words, leverage your earlier jobs to get you into better, higher paying jobs. Also, note how extracurricular activities can add solid weight to your resume as it did his. Note that the types of extracurricular activities on his resume helped him to acquire his last two jobs.

Refrain From Job Descriptions, Duties, and Responsibilities

As I did not help my son build his resume, he has some things on there that I would have done differently. However, generally speaking, he created some bullets that are accomplishments, achievements, performance, and results. These are what "grab" the reader's attention. I encourage you to do likewise. Refrain from making bullets that are job descriptions, duties, and responsibilities.

Good luck on building an attractive, compelling, and impressive resume! If you do that, your resume will generate many calls for interviews.

Education

2003   **BRIGHAM YOUNG UNIVERSITY**   PROVO, UT

Bachelor of Science in Accounting, second major in Korean (GPA: 3.59)

- President, Management Society Campus Chapter and Marriott School Dean's Student Council
- Vice President, Venture Capital Society
- Vice President of Public Relations, Beta Alpha Psi
- President, Korean Interest Association

Experience

2003-Present   **ERNST & YOUNG LLP**   SAN DIEGO, CA

Staff Auditor

Performs audit procedures on financial statement accounts for public and private clients. Analyzes and tests internal controls and business processes. Maintains client relationships.

2002   **PARTNERS GROUP**   NEW YORK, NY

Private Equity Analyst Intern

Completed various projects for one of Europe's largest independent managers of private equity investments. Screened potential investment opportunities and prepared first-level recommendations to the investment committee. Monitored existing private equity fund investments.

- Analyzed US buyout fund landscape and created marketing tool that compares track record and quality of private equity managers throughout the industry.
- Contributed significantly by performing fund analysis of two private equity portfolio mandates.
- Researched and reported on hedge fund penetration to U.S. affluent investor market and U.S. fund-of-hedge-funds products.

1999-2001   **PMG, INC.**   PROVO, UT
Vice President of Sales and Marketing

Managed over 20 sales employees. Implemented sales strategies and directed operations.

- Led sales team to 275 percent increase in sales over previous year.

Senior Sales Representative

Sold tax strategy and estate planning legal packages for regional law firm.

- Generated over $200,000 revenues and earned recognition as the top producing sales representative.
- Promoted to Vice President of Sales and Marketing for successes.

1999   **HAWAII STATE LEGISLATURE   HONOLULU, HI**
Legislative Assistant

Satisfied constituent inquiries in person and in writing. Prepared memorandums and performed computer-related tasks for the State Representative.

Project Manager

Organized and led a network of over 450 co-workers in the House of Representatives during month-long food-bank drive. Created seven large-scale fundraising activities with successful constituent participation.

- Collected 50,000 pounds of food, which increased food donation by over 250 percent of prior food drive.

Writing Bullets With Impact

I was wondering if you could help me with the wording of the following item that I have in my resume. This is how I have it in my resume now: "Led and ensured time sensitive projects were completed accurately and on time." This is what I want to say, but it is not in good resume language.

I have led teams of coworkers in projects (such as Reduction in Force) that are very time sensitive and require information to be accurate. People's jobs and livelihood are in jeopardy. If mistakes are made, someone could lose their job. How do you think I can word it? Any ideas?

Make Bullet Statements Quantitative and Measurable

This is your bulleted statement that you wanted me to improve: "Led and ensured time sensitive projects were completed accurately and on time." A statement like that is too terse, nebulous, vague, and qualitative. You need to make it more specific, quantitative (if possible), measurable (if it is quantitative, it will be measurable), significant, and full of impact.

Create Bullets That Make Sense

Saying "Led and ensured time sensitive projects" does not make sense. You can "lead a time-sensitive project," but I do not know how you can "ensure a time-sensitive project." Hence, the two words together inject confusion in the sentence. However, you certainly can "lead a time-sensitive project and ensure that it was completed accurately and on time."

Improved Bulleted Statement

You can say the following: "Led the time-sensitive Reduction-in-Force Project, ensured its accuracy, and completed it on schedule." However, you need to make it more quantitative and measurable. Hence, we could write something like this:

"Led (as project manager) five coworkers on a three-month Reduction-in-Force Project; achieved 100 percent force-selection accuracy with no unwarrantable selections, thereby jeopardizing zero jobs and livelihoods; and completed the project five days ahead of schedule and within the $10K budget."

Create Truthful, Factual Bullets

Now, note how I added some quantitative, measurable information to the sentence. Granted, because I do not know the background facts of your projects, what I wrote may not be the truth. However, you know what the facts are and should use my example as a baseline to start from and insert the truthful facts. Then, your bullet will have more impact in your resume. Do all other bullets in a similar fashion.

Do you see what I am trying to teach you to do here? You have got to make your bullets "grab" the reader with "hooks" that pack a "punch." Now, go and do likewise.

Examples of Revised Bullets that Pack a "Punch"

In the corrections that you made on my resume, you suggested that I add more "punch" to my bullet points; however, I am having a difficult time coming up with any. Would you please provide me with some suggestions?

Without Punch: *Develop an incentive program to raise fiscal awareness in the city.*

What fiscal awareness? Is it to increase city revenue or to save money? What kind of incentive program is this? Will it be monetary rewards/awards? This bulleted statement is too vague. It does not say or mean much.

Improve its clarity by saying something like this, for example:

With Punch: *Raises fiscal awareness in the city by developing an incentive program that provides city employees and residents with a reward of 10 percent of dollars saved by creative cost-reduction projects and/or 10 percent of revenues increased through innovative ways-and-means projects.*

Now, I know that I may be way off the beam regarding what you actually are doing; however, what I am attempting to depict by my example bullet is that you need to:

- Provide more specifics
- Inject some measurability
- Show quantitative facts
- Add more "beef"

Without Punch: *Update city website (www.delmar.ca.us/).*
How about something like this:

With Punch: *Updates the city website on a daily basis with multimedia (sound, color, motion, and interaction) improvements that increased the number of hits by 200 percent in the first month alone with an average monthly increase of 50 percent over the past 12 months.*

Now, again, I know I made up these numbers. Only you would know the real facts that you can use in your revised bullet. However, what I am showing here is that the revised example now shows:

- More specifics
- Measurability
- Quantitative facts
- Much more "beef"

It now "grabs" the reader's attention, "hooks" him/her to read more, and "packs a punch" to motivate the reader to action, i.e., to call you for an interview. Do you get the picture?

Without Punch: *Handle multiple phone lines.*

This one could be "beefed up" to read something like this:

With Punch: *Handles five phone lines simultaneously, which increased personal productivity by 50 percent, reduced need for another employee, and reduced company expenses by 25 percent per month.*

Does this not pack more of a punch than just "Handle multiple phone lines"? The response by the reader to your bullet would be probably: "So what? Handle multiple phone lines. Soooo! Big deal!"

Without Punch: *Schedule appointments and manage cash register.*

This one could be "beefed up" to read something like this:

With Punch: *Schedules, on average, 50 appointments per day, brings in average revenues of $5,000 daily, and manages the cash register that balances 99 percent of the time each month.*

Please note again that, by showing you these examples, I am *not* telling you to fabricate untrue statements with all of these numbers and facts. What I am showing is the kinds of truthful things that you need to put into your bulleted statements that will make your resume stand out.

If you cannot create "beefy" statements that "pack a punch," then you need to reassess what you are doing on the job and start doing things that you can write about that is more than mere job descriptions, duties, and responsibilities.

You need to do things that result in significant achievements, noteworthy accomplishments, positive results, and outstanding performance. Do you understand what I am driving at here?

Without Punch: *Handled over 300 accounts.*

This one could be beefed up by writing something like such:

With Punch: *Handled and processed over 300 accounts that generated $950K in revenue and saved over $250K in unnecessary expenditures.*

If you look at almost every one of these bullets, you will see that they state only a "feature." What is needed to "beef up" each statement is to add "benefits." In other words, "Handled and processed over 300 accounts" would be the "feature." Then, "that generated $950K in revenue and saved over $250K in unnecessary expenditures" would be the "benefits" of performing the "feature."

Without Punch: *Maintained low days to sales outstanding.*

This statement is not clear. It is confusing. Does it mean, "Maintained low days-to-sales outstanding"? Does it mean "Maintained low-days to sales outstanding"? Does it mean "Maintained low-days-to-sales outstanding"? For the want of properly placed hyphens, confusion is injected into the statement. Please clarify it with the proper placement of hyphens and add the "benefits."

Without Punch: *Researched stocks and increased volume of clients by networking.*

This one can be "beefed up" by writing it as such:

With Punch: *Researched 500 stocks and increased volume of clients by 200 percent by networking with over 1,000 new contact nodes.*

Now, redo your bullets by creating factual features and benefits that are real for your business.

Without Punch: *Attended and prepared for financial advising seminars.*

This one can be beefed up by rewriting it as such:

With Punch: *Prepared handouts for, attended, and supported the conduct of 40 financial advising seminars, which brought in 500 new clients and $2 million in revenue over a six-month period.*

Again, I know that my rewrite may be way off the beam as far as the facts of the matter are concerned. However, again, I am only trying to show you what we mean by "beefing up" your bullets. You know what represented reality in the firm at the time you had worked there. You know what kind of features and benefits you can create for your updated and improved bullets. So, armed with that knowledge, go and do the best you can in creating better bullets for your resume.

Without Punch: *Provided excellent customer service and trained new employees.*

What does "excellent" mean here? Do not use these kinds of vague terms that keep the reader guessing. "One person's *excellent* is another person's *poor*." So, avoid using *all-inclusive* or *all-exclusive* adjectives. Try something like this:

With Punch: *Provided customer service that kept, on a weekly average, 98 percent happy customers and trained 50 new employees over a two-year period.*

Do you see how you can quantify your bland bulleted statements and add "benefits" to your stated "features"? The "features" are what you did; the "benefits" are the good, positive, constructive results of your "features." Do you get it?

Without Much Punch: *Suggested new products that increased earnings by 10%.*

Hey, this is the only one that had some semblance of quantitative-ness to it! The "10%" is a "benefit"! Great! However, here is how you can beef it up:

With Greater Punch: *Suggested to management the addition of 15 new products to the store's offerings; the suggestion was immediately implemented; and the new products increased the overall store earnings by 10 percent. Received a promotion and $1,000 bonus for this value-added performance.*

I am making up stuff here to indicate to you the kinds of things that can be added to your bullets if, in fact, these kinds of results had actually occurred in real life. Now, I hope you have a better idea of what I have been driving at about adding "punch" to your bulleted statements.

How Do I Improve My Resume?

My resume is very dry and does not really "pack a punch" mostly because I have not done or taken a job were I could really excel. Currently, I work at a clothing retail outlet. When I think of accomplishments at my job, I can only think of one thing, which is that I have consistently been an employee that obtains a lot of credit card applicants. Getting people to sign up for the retail outlet's credit card has many benefits to our store, which I could list in my resume.

Are there other ideas of accomplishments that might be developed for this job, that you may have seen other people use, or any other ideas that could be generated? Do you think that obtaining credit card applicants is something that I could expand more on in my resume?

Since my resume does not have much "punch," what are some good job positions and in what industries are they available for someone that is still an undergraduate? If possible, would you give me some ideas of positions in several industries where I could start looking or researching? I am not quite yet sure which industry I want to go into.

Regarding my resume, I know I am supposed to list "accomplishments" or things that I have done that "pack a punch" under the job title. However, should I still list job descriptions such as the task that I am assigned to do? In class, the instructor said that most people were doing that in their resumes. Is it okay to list it as one sub-topic or should they mostly be omitted?

We Can Excel In Every Job We Hold

Let us start from this premise: *We can excel in every job we hold.* Now, all you need to do is to look for the things you can do to excel and write about them in your resume. Let us take your clothing retail outlet job for example. Obtaining credit card applications is an excellent area for developing a bullet with "punch." For example, you could write:

> *We can excel in every job we hold.*

- *Acquired 50 credit card applicants per month…the highest of all employees in the store, which increased store revenues by 25 percent in a six-month period.*

Created Factual Bulleted Statements

This example gives you an idea of what you can do with obtaining credit card applications. You put in the factual numbers as you see fit and can verify. You can create the bulleted statement in any fashion you so desire since you know the information.

Areas to Create Bulleted Statements

You can also create bullets on the following areas at the clothing retail outlet:

- How much sales you generate.
- How much savings you created.
- How satisfied are your customers.
- Any projects or work performed above and beyond the call of duty?
- Have you been recognized for anything with an award or reward?
- Have you received any promotions, raises, or bonuses?

Seek Jobs You Can Sink Your Teeth Into

You need to decide what you might want to do for a career. Once you do that, then you can start researching the kinds of jobs that would interest you. You should seek the kind of jobs that you can sink your teeth into so that you could prepare bullets that "pack a punch."

Using a One-sentence Job Description Under Each Job Title

On your resume, yes, you can put a one-sentence job description under each job explaining what the job entails followed by two to five bulleted statements that accentuate your significant accomplishments, remarkable achievements, superior performance, and outstanding results.

Redline Changes

Remember, the cardinal rule is that *you should not include any suggested redlining changes you receive from anyone unless you fully and totally agree with those suggested changes.* That way, you will take full responsibility for the change. If you do not agree with or have doubts about a suggested change, do not make the change.

Save All Suggested Changes

However, I suggest you keep in a separate file all of the redline changes made on your resumes. If your resume fails to generate sufficient calls for interviews, then you need to re-assess your disregard of any of my suggested changes. By saving the redlined changes from previous versions, you will be able to refer back to them quickly and, perhaps, reconsider using them.

Disregarding Counsel

Some of my clients disregard many of my redline changes. Then, they find that they do not receive many calls for interviews. When they go back a later date and make the changes and then send out their resumes, calls for interviews come flowing in.

The True Test

Hence, the true test is this: If you disregard suggested changes but receive a good number of calls for interviews, then what you are doing is correct. The only "proof of the pudding" is how many calls for interviews you receive. If you obtain sufficient calls for interviews doing it your way, then you have made the right decision to follow your instincts.

Chapter 3   Cover Letters That Entice

Some hiring professionals won't even look at your resume if your cover letter has some typos. Your cover letter should show the quality of your work, your attention to detail, and the results you expect from yourself and others. Therefore, your cover letter must be perfect, nothing less. Pay close attention to grammar, punctuation, and spelling. In this age of technology, there is no excuse for typos.[3]

Joe Hodowanes
Career Strategy Advisor
J.M. Wanes & Associates
www.jmwanes.com

Cover Letters are Sales Documents

Like the resume, cover letters are sales/marketing documents. The main purpose of cover letters and resumes is to generate calls for interviews. If they do that, you have an effective cover letter and resume.

Test the Waters

Yes, once you prepare a good cover letter, you are at a point to start sending out your resume to "test the waters." If it does not generate calls for interviews, then you need to go back and "beef it up" some more. In the meantime, continue to tweak and iterate your resume to continuously improve it.

---

[3]   Joe Hodowanes, "Cover Letters: The 13 Biggest Mistakes to Avoid," Letter Resources (North Chelmsford, MA, Net-Temps, Inc., http://www.net-temps.com/, 2004), visit Joe's website at http://www.jmwanes.com.

Purpose of the Cover Letter

Like the resume, you need to develop a "Wow!" of a cover letter. The cover letter is the same as your resume. It is a sales/marketing document. Like the resume, the only purpose of the cover letter is to generate calls for interviews. So, as you prepare your cover letter, keep those things in mind. Your cover letter must also "pack a punch" and should have "hooks" that "grab" people's attention. Go do it!

Typical Areas for Improvement in Cover Letter Writing

Your Address Block

Place your address block at the top center of the page to form a letterhead. Make it attractive and presentable. Include your name, address, phone numbers (work—if allowed, home, and cell), fax number (if you have one), and email address.

Addressee's Address Block

Include the name and title of the person you are writing to, his/her business address, and date. The date of the letter should be placed between Your Address Block and the Addressee's Address Block. You should usually allow at least a space between Your Address Block and the date and one space between the date and the Addressee's Address Block.

Salutation

Include the name of a real person in the salutation. Do not put the first and last name of the person in the salutation. Do not say "Dear Gino Fontana" or "Dear Mr. Gino Fontana." Instead, say, "Dear Mr. Fontana."

Requirements vs. Qualifications Table

If you prepare a "Your Requirements vs. My Qualifications" comparison table, matrix, or bulleted list, make sure your comparison lines up line for line or bullet for bullet. Do not make it into a "Try to match the requirement to the qualification game." In addition, do not say that you have a good or perfect match when looking at the corresponding bullets show very little matching whatsoever or even poor matching. Do not do that! It just tarnishes your credibility. If you lose credibility on the cover letter, the reader may never flip the page to look at your resume. So, construct your letter with integrity.

The Use of "I"

"I" may be used in the cover letter, but it should never be used in the resume. In the cover letter, however, several consecutive sentences should not start with the word "I." Similarly, several consecutive sentences should not start with the word "My." Mix it up a bit. Too many "I's" or "My's" make you sound too self-centered and egotistical.

All-Inclusive and All-Exclusive Words

Avoid (like the plague) using all-inclusive and all-exclusive words in both your cover letter and resume. All-inclusive words include excellent, outstanding, superior, world-class, genius, all, total, thorough, exceptional, superb, terrific, best, and top. All-exclusive words include no, none, wrong, ignorant, empty, zero, zilch, nada, worthless, ineffective, loser, nothing, worst, bad, evil, idiot, and hate. These words get you in trouble with the reviewer and/or interviewer. Too many students use these dangerous kinds of words in cover letters and resumes.

Abbreviations and Acronyms

When you use an abbreviation or acronym for the first time, define it. Just because you know what "SIE" stands for, that does not mean everyone else reading your resume would know what it stands for also. Indiscriminately using "alphabet soup" in your cover letter and resume is not a good idea. Make sure your cover letter and resume leave no question in the reader's mind.

Make your two most important sales documents (your cover letter and resume) easily readable and understandable. Within the body of your cover letter, spell out the states you use. Do not use the usual abbreviations, e.g., CA, NY, WY, etc. Spell out "CA" as "California." You may use "California" in its abbreviated form, i.e., "CA," in your address blocks and throughout your resume. However, do not abbreviate state abbreviations as "Ca," "Ny," "Wy," etc. Spell it in all caps as required by the Post Office Department.

Don't Beg

Do not start a sentence with, "Please consider me for the Associate Marketing Manager position…." Do not appear to be begging for a position. After all, you are bringing a lot of talent, education, energy, and experience into doing a superb job as Associate Marketing Manager for the hiring company.

If you sound like you are begging, you will place yourself in a disadvantageous position when it comes to negotiating the best salary and benefits possible. Be positive, dynamic, proactive, confident, and assured in your writing, speaking, and mannerisms. Project a positive image in both writing and in person.

Number of Paragraphs

Your letter should have three or four paragraphs to it, not just one paragraph. Do not go over one page on your cover letter. As your first "real" job out of college, never go to a two-pager.

The first paragraph should indicate why you are writing to the addressee. State the position you are applying for and what ad source to which you are responding. State as to why you are interested in the vacant position.

In the second paragraph, state your qualifications, experience, education, and bulleted significant accomplishments relevant to the job.

The third paragraph should focus on the hiring company. Do not just extol the virtues of the company. They know how good they are and how attractive they are to job seekers. *Tell them what you will be doing for them.* Tell them how you will make their company grow, become more productive, triumph over their competition, and become more efficient and effective.

In the final paragraph, invite them to review your attached/ enclosed resume. *Tell them how much you want to go to work for them.* Close with an invitation for them to call you at your phone number. In addition, tell them that you will be calling them in a week-to-10 days to set up an appointment if you do not hear from them by that time.

> *Tell them what you will be doing for them.*

Closing

Close your letter with "Sincerely," "Sincerely yours," or something similar. The "Sincerely" should be placed on the bottom left side one space from the last line of the last paragraph of the body of the letter. Leave two to three spaces between the "Sincerely" and your name. Finally, leave yourself enough space to write your signature in that space without being cramped.

> *Tell them how much you want to go to work for them.*

Make 'em READ Your Cover Letter Using This Killer Secret!

"*Got your attention? Great. That was my intention. Who wouldn't want to read on when the title promises a 'killer secret'?*

If I hadn't nabbed you in the first three seconds; however, I'd have lost you. People read and decide just like that. A job interviewer does the same thing. Read and toss. Read and toss. But that doesn't have to happen to your cover letter. You can grab and keep his or her attention with a smashing title or headline. This technique is one of the best-kept secrets in the career industry. Most job-hunters focus on their credentials, instead of focusing on the hiring manager they want to meet in person. Make him or her read your complete cover letter from start to finish without blinking."[4]

---

[4] Jimmy Sweeney, president of CareerJimmy and author of the new *Amazing Cover Letter Creator*. Net-Temps *CROSSROADS JobSeeker News*, URL: www.nettemps.com/adcgi/banner.cgi?ref=crnews&ch=1535&id=crs_1535

Use an Effective Cover Letter

Here is an outstanding cover letter prepared by Sarah Boyd. The letter is attractive, concise, and to the point. She covers the job requirements and how her background meets those requirements. A cover letter should accompany every resume you send out. It is a great cover letter!

Sarah Elizabeth Boyd

5420 San Marcos Boulevard
San Marcos, CA 92069

Home Phone: (760) 752-3697
Cell Phone: (760) 758-1234
Email: sboyd@adelphia.net

February 28, 2005

Mrs. Linda Baughman
President and CEO
USE Credit Union
10120 Pacific Heights Blvd.
San Diego, CA 92121

Dear Mrs. Baughman,

During a recent visit to the career development section of USE Credit Unions website, I noticed a need for a Branch Manager at the Berkeley location. My experience working on the frontline of branches, working in a back office role, and with the near completion of a B.S. in Business Administration degree enables me to bring significant knowledge and experience of the job at hand. Please consider me for the Branch Manager position, as I would be an asset to USE Credit Union.

Your position identified several requirements that fit extremely well with my qualifications.

YOUR REQUIREMENTS	MY QUALIFICATIONS
• Four year college degree or equivalent level of experience.	• Bachelor of Science in Business Administration.
• Previous financial institution experience.	• Four consecutive years of working in a financial institution.
• Communication and sales skills.	• Six years of communication and sales experience.
• Self-motivated.	• Highly motivative and striving to make a positive impact.

I am confident in my knowledge and experience to make a positive contribution to USE Credit Union. I am enclosing my resume for your further review. If you have any questions or would like additional information, please contact me at sboyd@adelphia.net or by phone at (760) 752-3697 (home) or (760) 758-1234 (cell). I will contact you next week to request an interview. Thank you for your consideration in reviewing my application.

Sincerely,

Sarah Elizabeth Boyd

Examples of Two Other Good Cover Letters

On the following two pages, we show a couple of good examples of cover letters written by college students. Note that there is no standard, universal, best way to prepare a good cover letter.

Jeremy J. Johnson

10078 Paseo Montril #712	Home: (858) 538-6990
San Diego, CA 92129	Fax: (858) 538-6990
Jeremy@pedalpusherpedicabs.com	Cell: (619) 384-2453

April 10, 2004

Kinko's Inc.
Three Galleria Tower
13155 Noel Road, Suite 1600
Dallas, TX 75240

Dear Ms. Berglas:

During a recent visit to careerbuilder.com I noticed an opening for a branch operations manager through your leadership development program. This career opening attracted my attention because I feel that I have the proven skills that you would be looking for in order to fill this position.

Your position announcement identified several requirements that fit extremely well with my qualifications.

YOUR REQUIREMENTS	MY QUALIFICATIONS
• Four year college degree, or equivalent level of experience	• Bachelor of Science in Business Administration with an emphasis in Service Sector Management to be awarded in December 2004 from California State University San Marcos.
• One-to-three years of related experience, prior supervisory experience required	• Nine years of direct supervisory experience of employees and subcontractors while operating two personally owned small businesses
• Advanced level of reading, writing, and mathematical ability	• Currently working on Bachelor on Science in Computer Science. Fulfilled 2,500 word writing requirement in each upper division courses.
• Proven ability to communicate effectively with team members and customers	• Conducted training for new employees and offered informational sightseeing tours for customers
• Proven ability to lead, direct, and supervise	• Held several leadership positions in campus and private organizations

Having contract work for Kinko's during their 1998 manager's convention in San Diego, I became aware of the excellence that Kinko's aspires to and the incredible culture of the company. Your core values of teamwork, respect, passion for results and community involvement are shining examples of why Kinko's is a corporation in which I would like to work. In addition, I foresee much greater opportunities for Kinko's in the future with its recent affiliation with FedEx.

Because of the importance of this position and the need to be filled in a timely manner, I will be contacting you in the next few days in order to arrange for an interview at a time that would be convenient for you. If you have any questions or desire any additional information, please feel free to contact me at johns215@csusm.edu or by phone at (619) 384-2453. Thank you for your time and consideration that you and the other staffing managers will give in reviewing my application.

Sincerely,

Jeremy J. Johnson

Jeremy J. Johnson

The bottom line to good cover letter writing is if your cover letter (along with the resume) generates calls for scheduling interviews with you; then it is a good cover letter. Your cover letter has sold the hiring manager to motivate him/her to read your attached resume and ultimately to schedule you for an interview.

Michael W. Turner

1077 Treadwell Avenue - Simi Valley, CA 93065-5039 - (619) 925-9039 - turne038@csusm.edu

February 23, 2004

Mr. David Pitts
Hiring Manager
Centex Corporation
2728 North Harwood
Dallas, TX 75201-1516

Dear Mr. Pitts:

This letter responds to the assistant Project Manager position advertised on the Centex website. I am familiar with your Fortune 500 organization and its reputation for being a leader in the home building industry and am certain that my education and experience would complement Centex Corporation's tradition of excellence.

My resume indicates that I am currently completing my bachelor's degree in Business Administration at California State University San Marcos. While I learned the foundations of financial theory through my coursework, consulting gives me the opportunity to apply this education to real-life situations. Consulting helps me develop effective time management, communication, and leadership skills critical to successful managers.

I want the opportunity to demonstrate my financial skills relevant to land acquisition. I will call you by telephone within the next week to discuss how I will help your organization grow. Thank you for your time and consideration.

Sincerely,

Michael Turner

Enclosure

Chapter 4   Resume Mechanics

We all want to make it to the top of that teetering pile of resumes atop hiring manager's desks. Competition is fierce. Here are a few secret insider tips that can help you get picked as the top candidate every time.

*1) **Be Bold:** Think of your resume as a one-page billboard. Lots of white space, bold bullet points, and get rid of that vague objective. Quantify your accomplishments with numbers where you can.*

*2) **Be the Perfect Fit:** Mirror the ad's language in your cover letter and resume. Many companies use software that looks for key words to identify top candidates, usually those are the same words in the ads. Even if they do it the old-fashioned way, it will make you look like a perfect match.*

*3) **Avoid the No.1 Mistake:** Make sure your language exudes confidence. Too many candidates sound like they are asking or even begging for consideration. You are not asking; you are making them aware of all the wonderful things you have to offer. If you're not excited about what you have to offer, why should they be?*[5]

Cynthia Shapiro
Career Coach and Author
CorporateConfidential.com

Typical Areas for Improvement in Resume Writing

Degree

Don't give the impression that you have already graduated with a degree. If you have not yet received your degree, always state something to the effect that you

---

[5]   Cynthia Shapiro, "Insider Tips to Put Your Resume on Top," *The Career News*, Vol. 5, Issue 38, September 26, 2005.

will be graduating in May 2005 or December 2005. Know your degree! Write your degree title down correctly. Some students don't even know what degree they are receiving because they had presented it incorrectly.

Consistency Between Letter and Resume

Make sure you use the same job title in the cover letter as in the resume. Showing different job titles in the cover letter and resume makes you look like you don't know what you are doing. If you use your grade point average (GPA) in both your letter and resume, make sure that they are the same on both pages. Too many students show different GPAs in the letter and resume.

Another thing, do not use a different month of graduation going from your cover letter to your resume. One person had August 2005 in the cover letter and May 2005 in the resume. Go figure! That demonstrates lack of attention to detail. Pay attention to detail and be consistent in everything you do.

Job Objective

In the Objective, always include the job title and company to which you are applying. Do not use a generic objective statement. Your objective statement should be different for every job ad you apply to unless it has the same job title among different ads. However, the company name should be different in every case. What I am saying here is that you should customize and tailor your Objective for every job to which you apply.

One or Two Pages on Your Resume?

At what point do I go from a one-page resume to a two-page resume? The information that I currently have, if I adjust the margins, will not fit on one page. Therefore, I can either cut out more information or add more details and stretch my resume to two pages. What is your advice?

One page! Cut out the fat. When you have more than 15 years of experience, then, go to a two-page resume. Of course, if you accomplish 10 times more than your peers do at the same age, then you could go to two pages. However, not many people accomplish 10 times more than their peers. They would need to have *mucho* irons in the fire, 15 balls up in the air simultaneously, running as fast as they can run, and sleeping a very few hours a night. Not many people can do that.

When President Thomas S. Monson was called as a bishop at the age of 22 of a 1,000-member ward (congregation), that's what I call accomplishing 10 times more than his peers did at the same age of 22. Of course, people like that become prophets, presidents of major corporations, or presidents of their country. If you're that kind of person, go to two pages on your resume. You want to fill another page with "meaty" stuff, not just a bunch of fluff and fat. Do you understand?

Showing a Degree Not Yet Received

Under the education heading in a résumé, how would one list a yet-to-be-completed degree such as an MBA degree?

You should always tell the truth on your resume. Some students stretch the truth by indicating that they already have received the degree. That is a dangerous practice. If you are several weeks or months away from receiving the degree, you should always indicate that you are either "working on the degree" or that you will be "receiving the degree at a future date."

For example, here is what you can show for your education:

Education

- MBA degree, California State University at San Marcos, to be awarded in June 2006
- BSBA degree, California State University at San Marcos, 2001

Another way to show it would be:

Education

- MBA degree, California State University at San Marcos, 2006
  - Still working on this degree
  - Graduation date is June 2006
- BSBA degree, California State University at San Marcos, 2001

Never, never show it just this way (below) if you have not yet received the MBA:

Education

- MBA degree, California State University at San Marcos, 2006
- BSBA degree, California State University at San Marcos, 2001

That would be a flat out-and-out lie. However, I have seen some students show their education this way on their resumes. Don't do it. If you have yours shown this way on your resume, change it now!

Improving Your Resume

Cardinal Rule

My cardinal rule about revising or updating resumes is that the owner of the resume (i.e., you) must totally and unequivocally agree with any redline suggestion made by anyone (i.e., career center, class instructor, close friends, or anyone else for that matter) before you make the change. In that way, you take sole ownership for the change as though you came up with the idea and made the change yourself. After all, only you will either benefit or lose by making any suggested change. Does that make sense?

Margins

I suggest you always make a 1" margin around all four sides of the page. This suggestion, basically, is derived from my proposal writing, book writing, and technical writing background. I repeat, always, always, always make a 1" margin (top, bottom, left, and right) completely around the text of every page of every document you prepare in any course, field, or endeavor.

It is a standard convention. Hence, when you copy pages, the text or graphics do not get cut off. Further, when you bind the documents, the three-hole punch or spiral binding does not cut out text or graphics or obscure them in any way.

Cover Letters

Even when writing cover letters, the left and right margin should be at least 1.25" (which is the default margin for MS Word documents anyway). The whole idea is to leave more white space on a typical page as opposed to having it too cluttered. Clutter does not impress the reader.

Font Size

I recommend that you do not reduce the font size just to fit more text on a page. Instead, eliminate some text. Font size should be either 11-point or 12-point, but not less than 11-point, like 10-point for instance.

Differences in Suggestions for Improvement

Remember this: there will be differences in suggestions made by myself, college professors, career centers, library books on resume writing that you may borrow, and speakers at career or job-searching seminars that you may attend. Furthermore, different people provide different suggestions because they come from different backgrounds and experiences.

Certainly, there will be differences in suggestions from someone (i.e., me) who has 40 years of industrial experience than you would have from someone with advanced degrees and working primarily in academia. The career center experts will also have different experiences, knowledge, and suggestions because they are keeping abreast (on a daily basis) with all of the new developments, techniques, and strategies that they read about from the continually growing career and job search literature.

"In the Trenches" Experience

My experience, for example, derives mainly from conducting over a dozen major job searches over the past 40 years through changing times, industries, and career levels; different markets, companies, and economic conditions; and growing information base of strategies, tactics, and approaches. I derive my experience through actually being in the trenches searching for work through the many avenues available (i.e., Internet/websites, newspapers, magazines, job fairs, career centers, seminars and workshops, networking, and you name it…I have tried it).

Involvement in Career Coaching

I have also written and continue to write papers and books on this topic; conduct career coaching consulting sessions and job searching seminars; and teach career development in college. I served as an officer career manager in the USAF, held employment specialist positions in my church, and helped numerous people with developing and improving their resumes.

No Right Answer

Hence, my "in the trenches" trial-and-error research results and discoveries will, in some cases, be different from those of the career center, career experts, and job-searching neophytes. That is okay. Sometimes, there is no right answer…just some better answers then others.

Continuous Improvement Process

Regarding resumes, if whatever you do to your resume achieves or improves the purpose of it, which is to get you interviews, then the changes are good. If it does not help you to receive calls for interviews, then the changes are not good. Only you can decide to make the changes or not. Then you can test the resume to see if it works to attract interviews or not. Hence, improving your resume is a constant, on-going process of iterations, testing, tweaking, testing, and improving/testing.

"I" Trouble

The use of "I" is okay in almost any kind of good writing. However, do not over-use the use of "I" and do not start too many successive sentences with "I." Only in the resume should you **not** use the word "I." Normally, resume sentences should be started with an action word or verb (usually in the present tense for a current position and past tense for all previous positions). However, you can use "I" in the cover letter.

If you have too many successive sentences starting with "I," you can resolve that situation by rewording appropriate sentences by adding an introductory word or phrase such as "However, I will...." or "Nevertheless, I have...." or "Because of those factors, I brought...." Do you get the idea? That eliminates starting too many successive sentences with "I." Hence, the idea is to bury the "I" within the sentence. It makes the sentence sound less egotistical than if you had, say, five successive sentences starting with "I."

Resume Questions

Including Jobs on Your Resume

1. *I only included my current jobs on my resume. Should I include my other jobs as well?*

If you don't have too many jobs say over the past 5 to 10 years, yes, include all of your jobs. You don't want to delete jobs that would create a gap in your resume. It is better to have continuous work over the years without any gaps of months or, worse, years.

If you have a lot of jobs, use those jobs that particularly sell you in the job for which you are applying. If you have multiple jobs simultaneously, use the jobs that best support your case for applying for a particular job. Short-term jobs that last for weeks or a couple of months may not particularly help sell you to the hiring manager. If the jobs were consulting gigs, then, perhaps, it wouldn't look bad. Jobs held for less than one year do not look good on your resume. They give the impression that you cannot hold onto a job for very long.

A One-Page Resume

2. *How can I keep my resume to just one page?*

First, start with the attitude that you ***shall*** limit your resume to one page. The "rule of thumb" is that you should have one page for every 10 years of work experience. Therefore, for young college students, it would be a while before you should go to two pages on your resume.

> *The "rule of thumb" is that you should have one page for every 10 years of work experience.*

Next, only include the most important things in your resume covering:

(1) your name and contact information,

(2) job objective,

(3) your career summary,

(4) education,

(5) employment experience, and

(6) anything else that space would permit, e.g.,

   (1) professional affiliations,

   (2) awards and recognition,

   (3) publications,

   (4) anything else that would sell you for the particular job for which you are applying.

One way to keep from going over one page is to avoid writing a bunch of job descriptions, duties, and responsibilities. If you were applying for a secretary's position, the hiring manager knows what a secretary does. Hence, you don't need to tell him again all of the secretarial things you did on your previous secretary jobs. It is the same way if you were applying for a food server position, or a landscaper position, or a retail sales position. The hiring manager knows what each of those people does. So, keep to the significant things that will sell you.

For example, your bullets for each of your jobs should include only your achievements, accomplishments, performance, and results. That's it. Many job seekers do not have many of these "hooks," "punch," "grabbers," and "beef" that "wow" the reader to call them in for an interview. If that is the case, then keeping to one page is easy.

It becomes a problem only for those who are "movers and shakers," those who "make things happen," those who "add value" to companies, and those who are "go-getters." Then, the problem for them is to decide which of their great accomplishments, achievements, performance, and results would be most beneficial for selling them to the hiring manager. I like to work those kinds of problems.

Contact Information

3. Do I need contact information for my resume for my employers?

I believe what you are referring to here is a list of past company work references. It is a good idea to keep contact information of your current and previous employers and supervisors. When you fill out an employment application form, you will need this kind of contact information including your previous supervisors' names, titles, phone numbers, and email addresses. You will also need the company name, address, and phone/fax numbers.

Another thing that you should prepare is a reference list of people other than your employers. This list may include co-workers, close friends, college professors (critical in your case), professional friends in your field of work (executives and managers are good here), clergy friends, professional organizational officers/leaders, and anyone else who would give you a good reference.

Both of these lists of references mentioned above should not be included on your resume. You should have these lists handy just in case you need to fill out an employment application form while you are there for an interview and if your interviewer asks you for a personal/professional reference list. If you have these lists handy, it will impress the interviewer/hiring manager.

Including High School Information

4. Can I include in my resume honors, volunteer work, etc. from high school?

If you have nothing to include in your resume in these areas from accomplishments acquired while in college, then, yes, include those from high school. If you have accomplished these things in college, then limit any of your high school accomplishments to only very significant items such as valedictorian/salutatorian, homecoming queen, all-state sports, major scholarships, student body president, state science fair winner, eagle scout, etc.

However, if you have done anything worthwhile during your college career, you should be able to limit these items only to college accomplishments. If you are college homecoming queen, college valedictorian/salutatorian, All-American sports figure, Rhodes Scholar, Big Man on Campus (BMOC)/Big Woman on Campus (BWOC), *Who's Who Among Students in American Universities and Colleges*, and ASB president, then you won't need to include these similar recognitions that you may have accomplished in your high school career. What you should have accomplished in college should have superseded everything you did in high school.

Likewise, after your first 10 years in the work world ("the real world") beyond college graduation, you should be able to eliminate all of your college accomplishments with work-world accomplishments with the exception of very significant college accomplishments. Do you get what I am driving at here? You should always be doing better such that you don't need to go backward to sell yourself going forward. After you get into the "real world," you should get the following kinds of accomplishments: president of major professional organizations, inventions/patents, book/paper publications, Outstanding Young Men/Women of America, listed in many Who's Who publications, discoveries, and many awards/recognition in your field of endeavor.

Envelopes to Use When Sending Your Resume

When sending in your resume, what type of envelope do you use? Should I use a manila envelope (8X11) in order to avoid creases in the resume? Alternatively, should I just use a standard white envelope, where you fold the resume?

When sending your resume to hiring companies, do not use an 8"x11" manila envelope because I don't think that size exists. Instead, use a 9"x12" manila envelope. That size is the right one to enclose your resume that you copy on 8-1/2" x 11" bond paper. Using this size envelope allows you to mail your cover letter and resume flat without any folds in it. Hiring companies like this better because it is easier to make reproduced copies from flat sheets of paper.

Also, do not staple the cover letter and resume pages together at the top left-hand corner. When the hiring companies make copies, they need to remove the staple with a staple remover and, more often than not, tear the corner off the cover letter and resume. This makes your cover letter and resume look sloppy.

Do not ever use standard white envelopes to mail your tri-folded cover letter and resume. Again, this makes it difficult to run copies on a copying machine. Often the copies are cocked to one side or the other because the pages do not fit flat on the copying machine glass. In addition, there is no good way of running folded pages through the automatic feeder. Stay with large manila envelopes!

Alternatives to All-Inclusive and All-Exclusive Words

You have mentioned a few times that when we are writing our resumes, we should not use all-inclusive or all-exclusive words such as "excellent," "exceptional," or "world-class." Hence, I was wondering if you could give me some other suggestions for these words that you have used. I've used "proficient," but I wanted to know what you think works best to enhance my resume.

Yes, when you write a resume and cover letter, avoid using all-inclusive words such as: excellent, outstanding, superior, world-class, genius, all, total, thorough, exceptional, superb, terrific, best, top, etc. Unless, of course, if you can prove unequivocally that that word is true and factual when describing you, then you could use it. Other people, in their letters of reference on you, could use these words freely, but you shouldn't use those words to define yourself. Let others define you with these all-inclusive words, but don't you do it.

Also, refrain from using all-exclusive words, which may be words totally opposite from all-inclusive words. Keep from using words such as no, none, wrong, ignorant, empty, zero, zilch, nada, worthless, ineffective, loser, nothing, worst, bad, evil, idiot, hate, etc.

It is better to use words that give you an out or an escape hatch. When someone writes in her resume that she has a "thorough knowledge of computers," she is sure to be proven wrong when the interviewer asks her a difficult question. Moreover, it probably will be the first question about computers that she will not be able to answer! I hate it when that happens.

Someone wrote in their resume that they were an "excellent writer." Then, I immediately proceeded to find scores of errors on the resume. So, in proving the words "excellent writer" wrong, the resume quickly gets round filed. Don't use all-inclusive words! It'll knock you out of the running every time.

Here are some more toned-down words that can be used effectively in resumes that leave you an out: proficient, proactive, good, effective, creative, innovative, dynamic, outgoing, productive, efficient, flexible, calm, organized, competitive, tough, resilient, energetic, hard-working, serious, team-player, mature, broad-based, experienced, seasoned, well, positive, knowledgeable, inventive, focused, inquisitive, quick, healthy, open-minded, fair, willing, constructive, prolific, etc.

Instead of being an "excellent writer," be a "prolific writer." Instead of being an "outstanding worker," be a "productive worker." Instead of being a "world-class marketer," be an "effective marketer." Instead of being an "exceptional photographer," be a "meticulous photographer." Instead of being a "superior cook," be a "connoisseur-pleasing cook." Instead of being the "best actor," be an "accomplished actor." However, if you won the "Best Actor Award," then you can claim in your resume that you were the best actor for that particular year you had won the award.

Do you get the idea? Do not put yourself in a corner for the interviewer to nail you with a well-placed question. Always leave yourself an out. Do not claim to be "perfect" unless you were God. Do not say you are "loved by everyone," because someone will surely prove you wrong. That's not to say that anyone else cannot describe you that way. It's only when we describe ourselves with all-inclusive terms that someone out there will certainly prove us wrong.

Bolding and Underlining Titles and Section Headings

I am unsure as to why bolding and underlining section headings is a problem in professional writing. Every business project I have turned in has been formatted in that fashion, and the IB curriculum I teach at work also requests similar formatting. I was curious as to what your requirement was based on. If it is a personal preference, that is fine as well. However, I was just curious as to any other particular requirement.

First, I do want to say that even though there is a continuous effort throughout the writing world to have and follow some standards, there are always differences. We try to follow standards established by the following:

- Webster's dictionary
- *The Chicago Manual of Style*
- U.S. Government Printing Office *Style Manual*
- Modern Language Association (MLA) *Manual and Guide to Scholarly Publishing*
- Shipley Associates *Proposal Guide for Business Development Professionals*

There are hundreds and hundreds of other style guides that you can find on the Internet, and many of them differ on certain publication standards. Even among dictionaries, there are differences. However, almost every style guide agrees with certain standards. One of them has to do with bolding and underlining. For example, in *The Chicago Manual of Style*, 14th edition, page 54, section 2.18, it states, "Chapter titles and subheads should not be underlined or italicized." The Shipley *Proposal Guide*, page 108, states: "Use bold text for emphasis rather than underlining. Underlining is harder to read and looks outdated. Avoid overusing bold or any other emphasis technique. Too much emphasis means no emphasis."

I have written and published over 30 publications including being a published author of nine books. I've been in the proposal publications business for over 30 years. I taught a course on "Writing and Publishing" with the Cal State Office of Extended Studies. However, never have I seen any standard that says to bold and underline the same words. I am surprised at what you wrote, i.e., "Every business project I have turned in has been formatted in that fashion, and the IB curriculum I teach at work also requests similar formatting. I was curious as to what your requirement was based on."

I have given you my requirement above. Therefore, would you be so kind as to quote the standard style guide that your IB curriculum used and where in the style guide that says you should "bold and underline titles and subheadings"? I am particularly interested in your standardized source, section, and page number from which this standard was referenced. It really baffles me that a standardized source would make such a statement. [Ed. The person who wrote the above question to me did not respond to my request to quote the standard style guide to support his position.]

Should High School Activities Go On Your Resume?

I have heard that after high school, you shouldn't put accomplishments and activities from high school on your resume. However, I have relevant activities and work experience that could help me with some jobs to which I want to apply. These activities involved facilitating events, which is what I am interested in pursuing as a career.

College Achievements Should Replace High School Achievements

By the time you make it through four years of college, you should have acquired a lot of significant college achievements and activities (yes, even facilitating events) to replace your high school achievements/activities on your resume. Just as within the first 10 years of working in the "real world," you should have acquired tons of achievements and activities to replace all of your college achievements and activities.

Exceptions to the Rule

However, there may be some high school achievements and activities that are so significant or so pertinent to the jobs you seek. In those cases, it would be okay to keep them on your resume. Just as 10 years out in the work world, you may have college activities that are so significant or so pertinent to future jobs you seek that it would be okay to keep them on your resume. However, generally speaking, most previous life's experiences should be replaced by newly-acquired, more relevant activities.

Examples of Significant High School Achievements

Some examples of significant high school achievements and activities include the following:

- Valedictorian/salutatorian
- Student body president
- Major scholarship winner (like a full-ride scholarship or something like a $100K scholarship)
- All-American and/or All-State selectee in any of the sports
- Making the US Olympic Team in any sport
- Homecoming queen or any other major queen contests (like Jr. Miss, etc.)
- School science fair 1st place winner
- Highest GPA in the school
- Movie stardom
- Being a prodigy in any of the arts
- Being elected to the city council of the local community
- Eagle Scout
- Selectee to one of the military academies
- Any other major recognition (e.g., *Who's Who Among American High School Students*)

Examples of Significant College Achievements

Some examples of significant college achievements and activities include the following:

- Valedictorian/salutatorian
- Student body president
- Secretary-General of the Model United Nations (MUN)
- Rhodes Scholarship

- College Bowl winning team member
- All-American selectee in any of the sports
- Making the US Olympic Team in any sport
- Homecoming queen or any other major queen contest (Miss World, Miss America, Miss USA, or any Miss some-state-or-another)
- Scholastic Fellowship
- Highest GPA in the college/university
- Movie stardom
- Any other major recognition (BMOC, *Who's Who Among Students in American Universities and Colleges*, Heismann Trophy Winner)
- Running a side business that makes millions of dollars of annual revenue
- Being elected to city council or mayor of the local community

Examples of Significant "Real World" Achievements

Some examples of significant achievements in the "real world" include the following:

- Major political figure (president, senator, congressional representative, Supreme Court justice, secretary of a national department, governor, mayor, etc.)
- Major military officer (flag rank, major command position, etc.)
- Congressional Medal of Honor recipient
- Military pilot "Ace"
- Astronaut
- Major movie star
- Oscar winner
- Major professional sports figure and award winner
- Any of the Halls of Fame selectees
- Chief executive officer (CEO) of a major corporation, non-profit corporation, university, etc.
- 10 Outstanding Young Americans selectee
- Nobel Prize winner (Peace Prize, Medicine, Economics, etc.)

- Major invention/patent
- Horatio Alger Award winner
- Olympic winner
- Super Bowl winning team member
- Pro Bowl selectee
- World Series winning team member
- Most valuable player (MVP) Award winner in any sport
- Best selling author
- Any world record setter/breaker in all avenues of life
- Best in the world in any of the arts
- Responsible for any major discovery
- Fulbright Scholar
- "World Class" status in any life endeavor
- Very important person (VIP) status in any life endeavor

Chapter 5   Lying on Resumes is a No-No

Be Aggressive, But Truthful: A resume is not a time to be humble. Be proud of your accomplishments, highlight them, and make the hiring manager take notice. But beware: don't let your creativity get the best of you. Your statements should always be truthful and results-oriented.[6]

> Linda Matias, president
> CareerStrides and the
> National Resume Writers' Association

Lying On Resumes

A survey by HireRight, an Internet company that checked out the resumes of more than 200,000 applicants last year, showed that 80 percent of all resumes are misleading. Their results: 20 percent listed fraudulent degrees; 30 percent altered employment dates; 40 percent inflated salaries; 30 percent had inaccurate job descriptions; 25 percent said they worked at companies that no longer exist; and 27 percent gave falsified references.[7]

---

[6]   Linda Matias, "5 Hot Resume Tips," Net-Temps, Inc., CROSSROADS Jobseeker News, use the following URL:
http://www.net-temps.com/adcgi/banner.cgi?ref=crnews&ch=1457&id=crs_1457

[7]   South Florida Sun-Sentinel—Knight Ridder/Tribune Business News via COMTEX, February 24, 2003.

Some Things That Resume Fakers May Forget To Tell You[8]

- They did not graduate from the college listed on the resume but took a class or two there.
- They do not have the listed certification but are studying for it.
- They got fired from a previous employer not listed on the resume.
- They have a felony conviction.
- The number listed as a previous employer is not for a business. It is for a buddy who is ready with an outstanding reference.

Resume Liars

If a job offer is withdrawn from a person being considered because a factual lie was detected on his resume, then, too bad for that liar. Every suspected liar should be confronted and given an opportunity to prove whether he/she had lied on his/her resume.

Fairness

If a person admits to including the false information, then it becomes a fact, and the job offer should be withdrawn. However, if a person can prove with authenticated documents that the resume-checking company was in error, he should be able to make his case to the hiring company.

Human Resources (HR) Folks

There is no good excuse for taking the reputations, futures, and livelihoods of job applicants so flippantly. The employers should get competent HR professionals instead of all the inadequate folks they usually hire. That is why these substandard HR folks spawned an entire industry of headhunters, recruiters, employment agencies, outplacement firms, career centers, consultants, and job fairs.

Unfairness

In most cases, however, the offer is simply withdrawn without the hiring company giving the potential employee an opportunity to clear himself/herself from the accusation. If that happens, it is unfair to the potential employee, particularly if the hiring company only paid $25 for the investigation by the resume-checking company.

---

[8]   Ibid.

Inadequate Verification of Damning Information

How thorough an investigation can a resume-checking company conduct for only $25? That would be about 15 minutes of effort. They just go online and check existing databases to come up with discrepancies or make a couple of phone calls. They cannot do much checking. Even if they charged $150, that is only about an hour-and-a-half of work to acquire and verify the damning information gathered on a candidate.

Private Investigators and Investigative Reporters

Private investigators and attorneys, spend many hours and days investigating the veracity of information gathered on the accused or defendant in court. Good newspaper investigative reporters spend many days and weeks checking and double-checking the veracity of the "facts" that they gather about someone that they will be writing damning information about (*The New York Times*, *National Enquirer*, and other tabloids excepted).

Faulty Databases

Many databases are riddled with obsolete, incorrect, and inaccurate data. Thus, it should only be fair for the accused job applicant to come face-to-face with the HR person and show proof that the damning data gathered on him/her is incorrect. If the accused, potential hire "no-shows," then that would be *prima facie* evidence that the accusation is correct.

I remember once when I had my own company, I had checked my credit rating with the TRW credit system at that time. I was shocked to find the data on my company was riddled with obsolete, inaccurate, wrong, and false information. That colored my attitude towards these kinds of databases on people and companies.

Not All Investigative Firms Are Honest

If the accused, potential employee shows up and presents data supporting his/her case, then the resume-checking company needs to prove that they have accurate data. It is only fair for this to be a requirement on all resume-checking companies. However, I think that whatever the resume-checking company discovers, the hiring company takes as factual, true, and accurate. There are a lot of unprofessional investigative companies affecting people's lives out there…just as there are resume liars.

Job Seekers Taught the Wrong Stuff

Some say, "What most need to do is manage the accuracy and credibility of the resume content professionally." How can this be done when outplacement agency consultants and career center instructors teach job seekers to put their "best foot forward," embellish on and accentuate their positives, and stretch the truth on their resumes and during interviews? Job seekers do what they are taught in job search seminars and consultation sessions.

The Truth Is Avoided

What they teach you to do is not really you. For example, they tell the job seeker to dress professionally for the interview, but after he gets the job, he goes to work in sloppy clothing. They tell the job seeker to put on all this positive image stuff, but after he gets hired, he goes back to his negative ways.

They tell the job seeker not to say he was fired or laid off even if that was the truth. They tell him that he should say that they had a mutual agreement to part company or that he was downsized, restructured, right-sized, and all of those silly "politically correct" terminology instead of saying what really happened, i.e., he was either fired or laid off!

Fairness Is Required

We must remember that we are not only job seekers from time to time, but we are also employers (for most of the time) who have to establish the veracity of resumes of the people we interview. I think it is only natural that we would all want fairness whether we are a job seeker or a hiring manager. Hence, as a hiring manager, we should also check the veracity of the investigative company's background as you would your potential employee.

Including an Honor Society on Resume but with No Participation

When I went to MiraCosta College, I was part of Phi Theta Kappa, an honor society; however, I never attended meetings so, I really couldn't talk too much about it. So, should I list this association on my resume?—Leah Belmonte

If you have room for it on your resume, yes, list it. It is an honor to be in Phi Theta Kappa (PTK); so, you might just as well as include it. If you are concerned about the interviewer asking questions about it, go to the PTK website and bone up on the organization. You should at least know the organization's purpose and activities. Do not volunteer your activity level in the organization. However, if asked directly as to your participation, do not lie. Tell the truth that you were unable to participate much because of other priorities. Then, move on to the next subject.

Truthful Resumes Written With Limited Experience

Due to a limited amount of experience, some people may need to represent themselves through their resumes. How should they go about writing their resume, which not only makes them look "good" yet does not mislead the employer?

The first rule to follow is this: *Never lie on your resume*. Stick with the facts that you have earned in your previous jobs, and you'll never mislead your future employers. If you have only punched in your time and did nothing significant in your past jobs, then, by choice, you have minimized your leverage in preparing a resume that packs a punch, includes bullets that grab the readers' attention, hooks the hiring manager to call you in for an interview, and "wows" the reader. All you can do is to do the best you can with what you have.

> *Never lie on your resume.*

Remember, *you cannot make a silk purse out of a sow's ear.* If you have no accomplishments whatsoever that you can convert into compelling resume bullets, then you will not have a good resume. Consequently, you will need to work very hard to find a hiring manager who will give you a chance to prove yourself. If and when you find someone who will hire you, start from day one to work on performing spectacular achievements so that you will be able to create powerful bullets on your future resumes to acquire future jobs.

> *You cannot make a silk purse out of a sow's ear.*

You are not accomplishing anything significant if you do not receive any of the following:

- Kudos for helping others
- Letters of appreciation and congratulations
- Awards
- Recognition
- Rewards
- Raises
- Promotions

- Bonuses
- Perquisites
- Choice assignments
- Praise
- Expensive training courses

So, start doing things to receive the things in the bulleted list above. Then you'll be able to prepare great bullets in your resume. Good luck!

Employment Gap

After being employed for 10 years, how should one explain to a potential employer an employment gap due to a pursuit of an undergraduate degree?

You never go wrong by always telling the truth. Just place the employment gap on your resume showing you were attending college in pursuit of your undergraduate degree. This is one gap-filler that will not be detrimental to you. Hiring managers understand that going to college full-time precludes working at a job, particularly if you are simultaneously a homemaker with young children at home.

> *You never go wrong by always telling the truth.*

Some young, single, full-time students can hold part-time jobs working 20 to 30 hours per week. But they usually don't carry the additional burdens of those married, older, full-time students who are homemakers with young children to rear. So, the older, married, full-time student should never be ashamed to prominently show the employment gap on her resume.

Chapter 6   Resume Gimmicks

Using Gimmicks with Resumes

I was thinking about sending a "keepsake" like a pen, stapler, or a paperweight with my resume. I figured that if the pen, stapler, or paperweight is attractive that they might actually use it…and if I put my name on it, maybe that would score a few extra points for me? What do you think?

No, do not do it! Keep your resume application professional. If you were at a tradeshow trying to coax customers into your booth, then handing out these kinds of "keepsakes" would prove to be effective. However, in applying for a job, you want to avoid being "off the wall" and doing "too wild" things that would turn off the hiring manager.

It is okay to be creative and innovative if you were going after a job in a "far out" kind of company that welcomes "wild things." Wearing a Mickey Mouse tie while interviewing at Walt Disney Studios may not get the surprise reaction that you may receive interviewing with a Wall Street firm. Most stable, conservative companies do not look with delight on unorthodox practices. Stick with the sure, proven, and tried strategies and tactics in searching for jobs with normal companies.

> *Stick with the sure, proven, and tried strategies and tactics in searching for jobs with normal companies.*

However, if you want to learn things as I do, you can test case these kinds of ideas on companies for which you don't particularly want to work. These things might work in the goofy movie industry or other such industries that are loose, flexible, and that "let it all hang out."

However, for the best companies that you desire to work for, stick with the proven approaches. Keep thinking creatively and innovatively though. Some day, these ideas will come in handy and provide you with a lucrative return.

Chapter 7   More on Resume Bullets

Do you fall into the trap of trying to create the perfect resume? Like artwork, your resume can never be perfect. It is either effective—generating calls from prospective employers, and winning interviews—or ineffective.

Focus your attention on writing results-oriented accomplishment statements, the most important content on your resume. Whether you "grew" or "increased" sales is not the important information—how much you increased sales and under what conditions is. Never sacrifice accomplishments in favor of all-inclusive descriptions of responsibilities, companies or activities.[9]

Roberta Gamza, president
Career Marketing Strategist
Career Ink

What Does One Do If He Cannot Prepare Bullets That "Hook"?

On my resume, I worked for a long time to get the bullets to where they are right now. I understand your concept about "hooks," but as hard as I have tried, I could not extrapolate from my previous jobs information to make them hook much more than that. I haven't gotten any specific accolades from employers (I haven't worked at a place where they did that yet), and I don't have any information on specifics on how my performance contributed to the company such as "Implemented new e-commerce store, which increased company revenues by 50 percent." I have read the chapter in your book on resumes over and over. Is there anything else I can do?

If you have really tried hard to develop meaningful bullets, then you probably do not have significant accomplishments that would generate good bullets. What

---

[9]   Roberta Gamza, "In Search of the Perfect Resume," *The Career News*, Vol. 5, Issue 16, April 18, 2005.

that indicates is that your current bullets are the best that they can be with what you have done in the past. So, you will need to look to the future.

In all future jobs, make sure you constantly have on your mind as to what you do and can do to generate good bullets that "hook" the reader, "add value," "grab" the evaluator's attention, pack a "punch," and "wow" the hiring manager such that he/she decides to call you in for an interview. Of everything that you have on your resume, the bullets are what will sell you to the interviewer and motivate them to call you in for an interview.

> *"…generate good bullets that 'hook' the reader, 'add value,' 'grab' the evaluator's attention, pack a 'punch,' and 'wow' the hiring manager such that he/she decides to call you in for an interview."*

If you strive for accolades, rewards, awards, and commendations, you will receive some of them, which would help you develop some really good bullets in the future. On the other hand, if you don't strive for these honors, you probably will not receive many of them at all. Like good goal setting, if you don't target things and go after them, they seldom if ever will just fall into your lap.

Plan your future and implement your plan. Set goals. Work towards those goals. As you accomplish your goals, you will be recognized for your good work. Now, you will have the ammunition to prepare bullets that pack a punch. Now, you will blow away your competition and receive those calls for interviews. Do it!

Don't Fight Creating Good Bullets

Some students fight using bullets in their cover letters and resumes. Some do not include a single bullet in their cover letter/resume. I don't know what it will take to convince them of the importance of strong, "beefy" bullets that "pack a real punch."

Why they "fly in the face" of all resume experts by discounting preparing hard-hitting bullets for their cover letters and resumes is beyond me. Is it because they cannot write a good bullet? Maybe.

If you really expect to be competitive with all those who write good bullets, there will be a "no contest" in that competition. You will lose every time.

Why write down the job description, duties, and responsibilities of a server, administrative assistant, or retail sales clerk? Everyone interviewing you for those jobs knows exactly what those kinds of workers do. Hence, why take up valuable resume real estate space writing the obvious? Instead, write about things that would interest and motivate them into calling you in for an interview!

Examples of Good Bullets

The following fantastic bullets were taken from resumes of students in my classes. If you learn anything about writing good resumes, learn how to prepare good bullets from these examples below. You can do it!

1. Single-handedly coaches 8 to 15 children ages 7 to 13 each session allowing for the club to cut costs to $10 per session and raise demand by approximately 20 percent.

2. Accredited with scores of 90 out of 100 and above during biannual reviews for outstanding performance.

3. Worked with approximately 50 special needs children of various ages increasing hands-on training by 25 percent.

4. Attended nine training sessions and received recognition as being the outstanding novice.

5. Implemented a marketing/advertising campaign, which increased sales by 20 percent. [attaching a dollar value would give the percentage an even greater impact]

6. Used credit union procedures to research possible fraud accounts that decreased total accounts by 10 percent.

7. Increased sales in San Diego territory by 15 percent in 2004. [attaching a dollar value would give the percentage an even greater impact]

8. Scored 100 percent by a secret shopper on serving skills and awarded a $50 gift certificate.

9. Created a 24-day "Teambuilding and Future Leaders" program for a charter school in Colton, California, which resulted in a school-wide change in attitude and respect.

10. Honored with corporate awards for outstanding performances with Wells Fargo including Top Performer in the Market Area 2001-2002.

11. Honored with "Super Nova," the most prestigious award for Wells Fargo.

12. Generates over $50,000 for the company every month through sales.

13. Developed a new inventory system for a product line that had been in place for over a year in order to monitor more efficiently current stock, order timing, and reduce ordering of in-stock items by 75 percent.

14. Consistently met monthly sales goals of 40 new policies while maintaining current customers and scheduling annual reviews for policies.

15. Promoted from Sales Associate to Replenishment Specialist (with hourly rate change from $7.25 to $8.50 per hour) for exceptional performance.

16. Awarded a $100 Christmas bonus from the owner for being a "hard worker."

17. Recognized by management with the Employee Excellence Award in July 2001 for hard work, dedication, and job-related abilities.

18. Filed as many as 20 pounds of records in a given shift.

19. Met ticket sales quotas of 50 people per small concert, for seven concerts, earning revenue over $1,750 per show.

20. Awarded over 30 Cornerstones for going above and beyond the job description to make guests' stay memorable.

Good bullets are "beefy," pack a "punch," "grab" attention, "hook" the reader, and "wow" the hiring manager to call you in for an interview.

21. Recognized for highest sales per hour (SPH) of $145.

22. Achieved a rate of 7 percent of sales in return dollars in 2003 and 2004, when the company-wide average is 3 percent of sales.

23. Top home sales consultant for four straight developmental projects resulting in over $2,000,000 in revenue for the company.

24. Promoted to Marketing Director after 10 months and awarded with the Leading Sales Consultant of the Year Award (2002).

In your final resume that goes into your Personal Career Portfolio (PCP), you should show no bullets with simply job descriptions, duties, and responsibilities. Don't tell me you cannot write *good bullets* that *are "beefy," pack a "punch," "grab" attention, "hook" the reader, and "wow" the hiring manager into calling you in for an interview. Good bullets must be real, factual, specific, believable, quantitative, measurable, and time-phased. Good bullets include features*

Good bullets must be real, factual, specific, believable, quantitative, measurable, and time-phased.

and benefits. Good bullets consist of performance, accomplishments, achievements, and results.

You cannot write these kinds of bullets unless you do more than your job description, duties, and responsibilities. You must go beyond that and be a mover and shaker, make a difference, add value, and make things happen in your jobs and companies.

Those who are able to write these kinds of bullets are not just putting in their hours each day at work. They aren't just punching the clock. They aren't just sitting there twiddle their thumbs. They are in the arena competing for victory, the win, and success. They are dreaming up new ideas, discovering things, creating things, inventing things, innovating things, making things happen, and achieving things on a daily basis. They are the ones who are receiving the awards and recognition, promotions, raises, bonuses, stock options, benefits, perquisites, and best assignments.

> *Good bullets include features and benefits.*

> *Good bullets consist of performance, accomplishments, achievements, and results.*

If you are not one of these people, then you need to have a paradigm shift and start doing something instead of moaning that you cannot write a good bullet. You must do something first…before you can write a good bullet. Start from today. Make this the first day of the rest of your career and life. Do it now!

Chapter 8   Resume Templates

Resume Templates Not Recommended

Are you familiar with any websites that offer free resume templates?

No, I am not familiar with any websites with free resume templates. You can find out where they exist by going to "Ask Jeeves" at http://www.ask.com and punching in "free resume templates." However, personally, I am not too impressed with using resume templates. I do not recommend using resume templates.

Your Resume Needs to Reflect Your Personality

I do not think templates incorporate your personality into the resume. For example, I am sure many of your classmates used the same template to develop their resumes. I know this because I find many resumes submitted to me for review with the same format and words used! When you read several resumes that have the same words, it sounds hokey to me. I was not too impressed when several people's resume said that, "their qualifications perfectly matched the position requirements."

Disadvantage of Using Resume Templates

I strongly dislike the word "perfectly" because, in reality, none of their qualifications matched perfectly with the requirements. I do not know many people who can come up with the same words as others unless they collaborated with each other…or used the same template! As a resume reviewer, I am not impressed. I wonder if the real resume reviewers would be similarly depressed.

Using Standard Templates

For the personal career portfolio (PCP) cover letter, is it appropriate for me to take a generic template cover letter from the Microsoft website and modify it to make it work with the job for which I am applying?—Roman Bogomolny

Yes, it is appropriate for you to start with a generic template cover letter from the Microsoft website and modify it to use for your personal career portfolio (PCP) resume cover letter. However, I haven't yet found any template of either a resume or a cover letter that is better than what I can personally do myself as a tailored/customized resume and cover letter. It is up to you, however. You decide what is best for you.

Remember, the bottom line of all resumes and cover letters is this: Do they achieve their only objectives? And what are their only objectives? Of course, to get you calls for interviews. Remember, both resumes and cover letters are sales/marketing documents. They must sell and convince the hiring manager to call you in for an interview. Also, remember, every resume you send out should always be accompanied with a cover letter.

Chapter 9   Miscellaneous Resume Items of Interest

Begin Your Resume with Bold Strokes—Recognize that the opening lines of your resume must grab readers by the lapels and force them to keep going. Typically, that has to happen within the first 15-30 seconds. Otherwise, you'll lose out to more compelling candidates. Every time.

So, in the top 20 percent of page one, clearly tell employers what you can do for them and why you're the one to do it. Back your claims with specific facts and figures that are easy for busy readers to grasp—no puffy language or empty assertions, please.

When you do this, and fire off your big guns early, you'll be 80 percent of the way toward getting employers to read your entire resume…and call you for an interview.[10]

Kevin Donlin
President
Guaranteed Resumes

Family Business

I have a question regarding the resume. Currently, I am working for my parents' company/store since my parents are semi-retired right now. I was wondering, how should I write about this job on the resume? Further, should I mention to the interviewer that my current job is with our family business?

---

[10]   Kevin Donlin, "Change Your Job Search Strategy," *JobSeeker Weekly*, September 12, 2005.

Just write the truth about your job and what you are actually doing in the family business. Yes, mention to the interviewer that your job is with your family business. There is nothing wrong with family businesses, and there is nothing to be ashamed of about a family business…even a mom-and-pop shop, which, basically, is what yours is.

Reworking Your Resume When Changing Career Fields

How do you suggest I rework my resume if I were to decide that I wanted to move into project management? I am assuming it would be wise to list projects I have managed, but what other things do you suggest?

Do the Necessary Homework

You need to develop a very detailed document of every job you have held thus far in your career. List under each job all of the significant tasks, assignments, and projects you had successfully completed. After you have these detailed lists, then, you need to identify those tasks, assignments, and projects that are connected to or associated in any way with project management. From those relevant experiences, develop a separate resume that should look drastically different from your HR resume.

Preparing Separate Resumes

Throughout my career, I, myself, have prepared separate resumes for positions in engineering, operations, project/program management, proposal development, education/teaching, general management, career development, counterterrorism R&D, and others. You can do likewise. The average person will have about six different areas of specialization throughout her/his career. So, start yours now by creating another resume for project management.

Recapitulation

Now, to recapitulate, these are the things you should consider doing:

- Develop a separate PM resume.
- Earn a certification in Project Management.
- Network yourself into a job closely related to the PM on a project.
- Attempt to obtain a PM position related to the human resources industry.
- Volunteer to work on and do work on as many projects as possible.

Enhancing Your Resume

I have continually encouraged people to work consciously at doing things to enhance their resumes. Creating "hooks" and adding "punch" that "grab" the reader's attention are things that enhance your resume. Hence, what you suggest in the question above is a good thing.

One of the things that will certainly add a "punch" to your resume is acquiring certifications. Hence, earning a certificate in PM (whether it is project management, program management, or product management) would look good on your resume. However, if you are going to continue to work, say, in software quality assurance, that may not help as much as if you were going to work in project management, program management, or product management.

Out-compete Your Competitors

Having to reinvent yourself for each job is not because of you. It is because of your competitors out there. Just remember that your competitors are not the millions of people out there also seeking work. Your competitors consist, basically, of around 200 other people seeking the same position you are seeking. All you need do is to create one of the five best resumes of the 200 people (on average) that are also sending their resume for the position to which you apply.

Develop a Winning Resume

Making your resume stand out from the others is the reason why you need to tailor/customize your resumes. Not many people will go through the trouble of tailoring/customizing their resumes and cover letters. That is why most of your 199 competitors are "also-rans" and do not get selected to come in for an interview. This is a secret that not many people know about, but also not many people will accept and put into action.

Building Effective Resumes and Cover Letters

- The resume and cover letter are sales documents. Period!
- The only purpose of the resume and cover letter is to get you an interview.
- Keep your resume continuously updated throughout your career.
- Build resume bullets with "hooks" that "grab" the readers' attention, pack a "punch," and "wow!" them.

- Good resume bullets should be significant, detailed, factual, objective, quantitative, measurable, and "beefy."

- Good resume bullets should have both a feature and a benefit.

- Good resume bullets cover significant achievements, commendable accomplishments, superior performance, and outstanding results.

- Do not build resume bullets that mainly cover job descriptions, duties, and responsibilities.

What Should I Do if I Have a Low GPA?

I attended a job fair held on campus. I actually was disappointed with it because I was expecting more from it. There were a few companies in which I was interested. However, one company would not give me an interview because I did not have the GPA to qualify for an interview. I have been noticing that a lot of employers are asking me for my GPA. My GPA is close to 3.0. How do you get pass this problem?

I'm sorry you were disappointed about not getting an interview because of your under 3.0 GPA. This indicates to you how important it is to study hard and earn a good GPA, which should be around the 3.5 area.

I had an even more severe GPA problem than you have. My undergraduate GPA at the University of Oklahoma was 2.7! However, since I had "majored in extra-curricular activities," I was able to earn a lot of things to put on my resume that compensated for my low GPA.

For example, I had items such as five part-time jobs, president of four organizations on campus, Student Senator for two two-semester terms, cadet colonel and deputy wing commander of Air Force Reserve Officer Training Corps (AFROTC), and outstanding sophomore and senior cadet. Furthermore, I had other items such as Loyal Knights of Old Trusty (LKOT) secret honorary engineering society, St. Pat of 1965 (outstanding engineering senior), Big Man

> *Some students don't care about learning anything. All they want are "A's." It is better to get a "B" and learn how to think, reason, conceptualize, debate the merits of things, and gain a solid understanding of the subject matter. Then, you can use that knowledge to discover, innovate, create, and invent, new things, be a visionary, and gain wisdom.*

on Campus (BMOC), *Who's Who Among Students in American Universities and Colleges*, among many other things.

Hence, by my generating all of these "bullets that packed a punch," I was able to "beef up" my resume that "explained away" my lower GPA. So, if you have other things that you can put on your resume that will "explain away" your lack of a high GPA, you will be given an opportunity to prove yourself in an interview.

When and if you go for advanced degrees, work hard to get good grades. Then, you will preclude needing to deal with this problem in the future. A lower GPA could haunt you in years to come in your job searches, the schools you can attend for advanced degrees, and other things. I know. My lower GPA did impact me negatively in the earlier part of my career. It is still impacting me now on the schools I can attend for a doctorate's degree and the colleges and universities in which I can teach.

So, study hard and get those good grades. And don't forget to learn something while you are earning good grades. *Some students don't care about learning anything. All they want are "A's." It is better to get a "B" and learn how to think, reason, conceptualize, debate the merits of things, and gain a solid understanding of the subject matter. Then, you can use that knowledge to discover, innovate, create, and invent new things, be a visionary, and gain wisdom.*

Resume Enhancement Activities (REAs)

Continually strive to develop resume enhancement activities (REAs), which will help generate bullets that "pack a punch." My principal REAs for the past 60-90 days included:

- Acquired a six-week (1/20/05 to 3/3/05) proposal consulting assignment with L-3 IEC and made about $25K. Worked over 84 gratis hours.

- Completed proposals on the Small Diameter Bomb (SDB), Lockheed Martin Evolved Expendable Launch Vehicle (EELV), and Boeing EELV.

- Working to register Bob Uda and Associates (BU&A) to get my company certified as an 8(a)/SDB/HUBZone company.

- Went to the notary public to notarize my signature for the 8(a)/SDB/ HUBZone program.

- Finalized my sixth book, *The Third Resource: A Universal Ideology of Economics*, with the publisher, iUniverse, Inc., which hit the booksellers' websites in April 2005.

- Wrote my seventh book, *Career Quest for College Graduates: Developing a Successful Career by Leveraging Each of Your Jobs*, which should be sent to the publisher in the June timeframe.

- Completed another successful semester teaching SSM 445 "Career Development" course (spring 2005 semester) at CSUSM.

- Talked by long distance with Dr. John I. Choate, who lives in Connecticut, about jointly seeking funding for the new keyboard he has invented and on Carpel Tunnel Syndrome (CTS) research through the Small Business Innovation Research (SBIR) Program.

- Made an unsuccessful attempt to obtain a $500 mini-grant from the North County Higher Education Alliance (NCHEA) to establish a Counterterrorism Research Institute (CRI) at CSUSM. Failure was due to not being able to acquire a letter of support from the High Technology Management (HTM) Program at CSUSM. Quite a bit of effort went into this attempt.

- Researching info for online doctorate program at the University of Nebraska-Lincoln (UNL); plan to start this PhD program on Educational Leadership and Higher Education (ELHE) in 2006.

- Joined the Association of Assessment and Counseling in Education (AACE) professional organization.

- Applied for full-time, tenured position of Associate Professor/Counselor at Palomar College.

- Submitted nomination for award in the San Diego Section of the American Institute of Aeronautics and Astronautics (AIAA).

- Interviewed with three people of Epsilon Systems Solutions, Inc., in Mission Valley for position to head up the Marketing and Proposal System (MAPS) for the company.

I have listed all of the items that I have accomplished in three months to "enhance" my resume. Do you get the picture? If you are not actively pursuing and making a concerted effort to network (meet and get to know people and vice versa) and to accomplish significant things to add to and enhance your resume, you are being "left in the dust" by your competitors. If you don't actively do these things in your career and life, things won't just automatically happen. You must make things happen. Do it now!

Does a Resume Establish Your Image?

Does a resume with a variety of certifications and job experiences make an applicant look well-rounded or not a stable employee?

No, a resume does not establish your image. You establish your image. Your attitude and behavior establish your image. Your resume only documents your accomplishments and sells your image that you personally have created. You also establish your image through your personal branding strategies. Whatever you do that creates in others' minds what you represent to them is your personal branding. So, you fully determine what and how you want others to perceive you.

> *A resume does not establish your image. You establish your image.*

For example, if you want to be seen as a funny person and a joker, you do a lot of silly things to create that image in people's minds. If you want to be known as a serious, scholarly person, you dress, study, and carry yourself as an educated scholar. If you want to be known as a bully, you push people around. If you want to be known as an idiot, you do a lot of idiotic things like the Hollywood elite for example. If you want to be known as a serious athlete, you do those things that show your athletic prowess and also live as a good role model.

> *You create and establish your image. You are doing that every day of your life. Whether you realize it or not, you are creating an image of yourself to others.*

See, it all depends on what you want to make of yourself. You create and establish your image. You are doing that every day of your life. Whether you realize it or not, you are creating an image of yourself to others. Would you rather create this image in a haphazard manner, or would you rather create it in a methodical, planned, and sculpted manner? If you want to accomplish great and wonderful things in life, you must create your personal brand in a pre-planned manner. That way, you don't do things that create an image that may need to take years for you to undo.

Now, whatever you do that you place in your resume to document your accomplishments and sell your capabilities will create a picture of you. Depending on your accomplishments throughout your career, you can create an image of yourself on paper, i.e., in your resume, as a manager, executive, engineer, writer, educator, consultant, researcher, proposal expert, or counterterrorism expert. With my background, education, job experience, and accomplishments, I can create a specific resume for each of these positions for which I may desire to apply.

Now considering your specific question, yes, a resume with a variety of certifications and job experiences may make an applicant look well-rounded or unstable. However, it may also indicate that the applicant did not plan his/her career to show any kind of career path-goal. It may indicate a broad base of experience where the applicant may be viewed as a "jack of all trades but a master of none." If you had a variety of management positions, it could indicate that you have a broad-based management experience.

Well-roundedness or instability is a perception created in the eyes of the beholder. *One person's well-roundedness is another person's instability.* When you interview, how you carry and present yourself will determine if you are perceived as well-rounded or unstable. So, your resume does not establish your image. You establish your image in the interview.

> *First impressions are lasting impressions.*

Remember this: first impressions are lasting impressions. If you make a good first impression, the interviewers are likely to retain that image of you. If you make a poor first impression, it may be very difficult for you to recover from that poor image of yourself. So, start with a flawless, outstanding resume with compelling bullets and attractive cover letter. Then, bolster that with a superb phone interview. And, finally, nail it down with a convincing face-to-face interview.

How to Be Discrete When Searching for a Job While Employed

What should a person do if he/she is applying for a job while employed and don't want his/her current employer to know? Does he/she allow the company to contact his/her current company when asked?

If you apply for a job and don't want your current employer to know about it, you need to be discrete about what you do. For one thing, do not post your resume on any old job website. Any company can pay to have access to all generally posted resumes. Make sure that you post your sanitized resume only on those websites that will protect your privacy. Your sanitized resume does not show your name and also deletes or obscures things in your resume that could easily identify you. Another thing you can do is to work through a good recruiter or headhunter who knows how to be discrete.

When a company is interested in making you an offer, make sure you tell them not to contact your company. You can give them other good references that they can contact to verify the veracity of your resume and the information you gave them in the interview. The only time you should allow them to contact anyone in your current company is if your company already knows you are searching for work because you have been designated to be laid off in an upcoming massive company RIF.

Explaining a Firing in a Resume and Interview

If you were fired from a job in which you worked for over a year ago, how would you explain this time gap on your resume? How would you explain this time gap in an interview?

Everybody should be fired from their job at least once or twice in their career. I've been fired thrice and laid off four times over the past 40 years. If you are a vice president or above and are let go or laid-off, all that really means is that you were fired! Being fired is good. It humbles you. Remember, *no man or woman is an island.* Any organization can go on with or without you. So, *don't ever think or feel that you are indispensable or too good to ever be fired.*

> *Everybody should be fired from their job at least once or twice in their career.*

Never state in a resume that you were fired from a particular job. Leave the answer to that question for the interview. If you allude to being fired in your resume, it will surely be tossed into the round file (i.e., waste basket). So, don't put yourself at a disadvantage. Don't ever state on your resume that you were laid off and then explain why. That would be akin to shooting yourself in the foot.

> *Never state in a resume that you were fired from a particular job.*

For a job that you've held for over a year and got fired, just show the job in your resume as you would any other job. Include bullets of your best accomplishments in that job. Don't ever give the slightest clue in your resume that you were fired.

Then, when you get to the interview, don't ever volunteer that you were fired. Only if your interviewer specifically asks you if you were fired from that job should you ever address that subject. If you are asked if you were fired, just answer "yes" and then wait for his/her next question. If he/she asks you as to why you were fired, just say that you and your boss had different philosophies of how to do things, so he/she let you go. Then, immediately talk about another subject. *Do not dwell on any position from which you were fired.*

Getting a Job in the Makeup Industry with No Resume Experience

I have a question about trying to switch the kind of career I am currently in so that I can have at least a year of experience by the time I graduate with my business degree. I was hired on as a teller at San Diego County Credit Union at the age of 19 when I wasn't really sure what I wanted to do with my life. I have stuck with that job for the last seven years because I was continually promoted and made pretty good money. I am currently a loan and new account rep, and now, I really know that I want to be a makeup artist, and want to run my own business doing so one day. I feel like my business degree and knowledge with school will help with this, but I really don't have the makeup experience except for what I have done on the side on my own. I do have sales experience in my current job, which is helpful with the makeup industry since a large part of their job is sales. When I have done makeup for friends, family, and co-workers, they are always impressed and love the job I do. I just don't have the extensive training usually required for this kind of position. I feel if I was hired on somewhere, I would take off and do very well once properly trained. How would I go about getting a job or even an interview for that matter in the makeup industry with no resume experience yet?—Angela Smith*

This is a tough problem because the career field you desire to work in is highly specialized, doesn't have many open opportunities, and is difficult to gain the requisite experience. Thus, what you need to do is the following:

- **Acquire Experience.** Acquire as much of the directly applicable makeup experience that you can by doing the following:
    - *Self-Employment.* Start a sole proprietorship now and create a great makeup artist company name—start developing your own experience
    - *Freelance Work.* Continue to do makeup for friends, family, and co-workers and keep a record of the hours worked and the people you worked on. This work (even if unpaid or meagerly paid) will become part of your business. You'll be acquiring real world experience through an official organization.
    - *Makeup Events.* Hold your own makeup events. This will be part of your business too.
- **Networking.** Network extensively in the makeup industry by doing the following:
    - *Professional Events.* Attend makeup trade shows, conferences, seminars, workshops, and expos

- *Professional Organizations.* Join makeup organizations, attend their meetings, and serve in offices in that organization. Include the names of the organizations on your resume.
- **Publications.** Obtain makeup books, magazines, journals, and other publications and periodicals and read all of them to get super-smart on the makeup industry and in being a makeup artist.
- **Certification.** Search for makeup schools on the Internet and take short courses, get certified, and gain hands-on experience in their labs.
- **Internship.** Seek a makeup internship.
- **Fringe Jobs.** Secure part-time jobs working on the fringes of the makeup industry to acquire relevant experience and develop transferable skills. Jobs such as the following "may" (some of these may not be good because they are just wild guesses on my part and my not being a makeup artist expert) help you build up the kind of experience that would be useful in enhancing your capabilities and track record:
  - Actor
  - Artist/Painter
  - Barber
  - Color coordinator
  - Cosmetics salesperson
  - Cosmetologist
  - Costume designer
  - Dietician
  - Designer
  - Events coordinator/wedding planner
  - Exercise coach
  - Graphic artist
  - Hairdresser/hairstylist
  - Interior decorator
  - Manicurist
  - Masseuse
  - Model
  - Model maker

- Personal coach
- Personal trainer
- Photographer
- Physical therapist
- Sculpture artist
- Seamstress

My guess is that the makeup industry is a close-knit industry. You need connections to get a good job within that industry. Therefore, you will need to get to know prime movers in the industry and get them to know you. Extensive networking is the way to do that.

In summary, you not only need to gain the:

(1) Knowledge by:
   a.   Reading the applicable magazines and journals
   b.   Taking seminars, workshops, and specialized schools
   c.   Getting licensed and/or certified and
(2) Experience through:
   a.   Internships or apprenticeships,
   b.   Performing small freelance jobs,
   c.   Starting your own firm, and
   d.   Getting your first big break, but you also need the
(3) Exposure by:
   a.   Participating in makeup artist professional organizations,
   b.   Attending large public gatherings of these makeup specialists, and
   c.   Networking with those who can give you that first big break.

You might also write papers on the subject to present at makeup conferences and to get them published in makeup artist magazines and journals. Why don't you write a book on the subject and become an instant expert?

You have excellent sales and business knowledge and experience. Generally, the three years you had worked in a bakery and café, seven years in banking, and a solid college education in business administration all will help you to get a good job. However, you now need to get the specialized knowledge and experience in the makeup industry for you to get a good job in that industry. So, work towards that end by considering the things I have mentioned in the above list.

Tailoring Your Resume for a Small Niche Retail Shipping Industry

I grew up around a family business within the retail shipping industry. I have worked within this field for over six years, and I feel that I could possibly be a real asset for companies such as UPS, FedEx, and/or DHL. The type of job I am looking for is a sales position that is responsible for managing retail-shipping accounts similar to my family business. I really feel that I fit into a small niche that understands these types of customers. I was wondering how I could put a positive spin on my resume in regards to promoting my experience in the field for the past six years. Do you have any suggestions as to how I might do this?—Lauren O'Sullivan

You need to create bullets that pack a punch from your past six years of experience in your family business that will support your sales position in your identified retail-shipping niche. Accentuate your relevant transferable skills and experience. Join a couple of professional selling organizations to help build your resume and get involved in their monthly meetings. Run for office, get elected, and serve in positions and on committees. Take a certification course/program to build more credibility in this area. Get an internship. Do whatever it takes to build up your resume.

How Employers Look at Length of Time in Previous Jobs

I had a summer internship with Geico Insurance just this past season. The position started at a competitive pay, and originally, I was very excited that I landed the job before I completed my degree. Recently, I have decided it is not the job for me. I learned that I cannot stand staring at a computer for eight hours a day, and that a cubicle is an unhealthy place for me. I understand that I must take the time to find the right job for me, but I am concerned that if I spend the next five years looking for the right job, my resume will look like I cannot stay employed at any one location for a long period of time. How much do employers take into consideration the length of time you have been employed at previous jobs?

You should always attempt to stay in a job for at least a year but never less than a year. You come down the learning curve during your first year on the job. You are most productive during the second year. You should never stay in the same job for more than three years. So, after two years, start looking for your next growth assignment.

This does not imply that you need to go immediately to another company. You should find another growth job within the same company. You should continue in the same company as long as they either promote or transfer you into a better job within the company every two to three years. If you are unable to grow in the same company, then you should start looking for a better job in another company.

If you had a new job every year, employers do not look negatively upon it if:

- Each succeeding job was a promotion and demonstrated career growth
- You acquired more responsibility, authority, and salary with each succeeding job
- Each subsequent job title indicates growth

What you need to watch for is to show instability through receiving worse jobs with each job change, making less salary than before, and/or having less authority/responsibility in subsequent jobs. This kind of work record does not indicate growth and/or progress. It shows one or more of the following negative traits:

- You cannot hold on to a job for very long
- You are unstable and cannot stay in the same job for any extended length of time
- You are difficult to get along with
- You are quickly bored and are off to the next thing (flighty)

This is how it is in the corporate world. Plan your career and implement your plan so that you will be able to achieve the negotiating advantage (i.e., leverage) required to get your next better job. If you do not work to do this, you will have a haphazard career record.

How to Make Your Resume More Appealing

My sister wants to get out of retail, and I am helping her with her resume. I am having a difficult time with her resume since she has only had retail positions. She has been to college but hasn't yet graduated. She doesn't have an impressive resume, and I want to help her get a job OUT of retail. She has a son, and the hours that a retail job demands aren't healthy for her husband and son. She gave me her resume, and each position has the same descriptions. She has been in management, but her resume lacks

A LOT of spunk. In what ways can I make her sound more appealing? If you can help, that would be great. I want to help her with this as much as I possibly can.

For your sister to get out of the "hole" she is in, she needs to do the following:

- Become a go-getter like you are
- Work harder and smarter in her current job
- Get recognized
- Receive awards
- Receive promotions
- Be better than all her coworkers
- *Note:* She can find success in retail if she really wanted to
- Build up her stature in the industry
- Complete her degree and then go for further education
- Get her to buy and read my books on *Career Quest for College Students*, *Career Quest for College Graduates*, and *What Hue is Your Bungee Cord?* They are available on:
    - http://www.barnesandnoble.com
    - http://www.amazon.com
    - http://www.borders.com
    - http://www.iuniverse.com
- Start networking vigorously
- Get smart about job searching by reading, attending seminars, and researching on job sites on the Internet
- Go to a governmentally-sponsored career center such as North County Coastal Career Center (NCCCC) in Oceanside, the North County Inland Career Center in Escondido, or the Metro Career Center in San Diego and take "free" courses in computers and other topics
- Do a personal assessment using the Career Success Map Questionnaire (CSMQ) and Jung Typology Test (JTT)/Myers-Briggs Type Indicator (MBTI) to help identify her areas of interest and "passion"
- Prepare three Occupational Analysis Reports (OARs) on three jobs she would like to have
- Prepare three Situation-Action-Result (SAR) stories

- Prepare a Personal Career Portfolio (PCP)
- There are many other things, but I will stop here lest she becomes discouraged

You know about all of these things. It is not easy to be successful. However, one must have a great desire to accomplish and succeed if one expects to reap the rewards.

What is a "Vita"?

Regarding a question I received about a vita, here is what it is. According to Webster, a "vita" is "a biography or autobiography, often a brief one." Then, there is the "curriculum vita," which Webster defines as "a summary of one's personal history and professional qualifications, as that submitted by a job applicant; resume." Literally, it means a "course of life," where "curriculum" means "course" and "vita" means "life."

The term "curriculum vita" or "vita" is used predominantly in academic circles. In industry, we basically use "resume." I have seen "vitae" or "curricula vitae," which are the plural terms, of all shapes, sizes, and format. They have ranged from a one-page resume, to one-page biographies or bios, to several pages of your life history, to a 27-pager that I have, which is what I refer to as a "dossier." According to Webster, a "dossier" is "a collection of documents concerning a particular person or matter."

So, according to Webster, then, a "vita" is a biography or autobiography, a personal history and personal qualifications, a resume, and a course of life. However, the key terms in the definition are "brief," "summary," and "resume." Webster defines "resume" as "a summing up; summary; a statement of a job applicant's previous employment experience, education, etc."

Please note, however, that the cutting-edge resumes I talk about in this book for winning good jobs are *not* biographies. These state-of-the-art resumes are characterized by the following:

- They are sales or marketing documents
- Their only purpose is to get you interviews
- They include dynamic bullets that "pack a punch"

If, say, you are going to be honored at an awards banquet, and you were asked to submit a vita for that banquet, I assume what they are looking for is something they can either publish/print in the banquet program or use to introduce you immediately prior to presenting you the award, or both. So, my suggestion to you is to prepare a one-page (absolutely no more than one page) vita in prose (which is the ordinary form of written or spoken language). Recently, I saw in a press release the biographical information (or bio) of the newly appointed NASA Administrator, Dr. Michael D. Griffin. I have included below that bio on Dr. Griffin to give you an idea of a good bio that can be used for the banquet purposes. The bio basically covers the following topics written in prose:

- Current job position
- Previous job positions held
- Teaching, publications, and professional registrations
- Honors and awards
- Professional affiliations (membership grades and offices held)
- Education/degrees and awarding schools
- Personal (date/place of birth, hobbies, and certifications)

Though the date/place of birth and hobbies would go on a bio to introduce you at a banquet, you would never include your date/place of birth on a resume and would discuss hobbies judiciously on a resume. *Any hobbies shown on your resume must relate directly to the job for which you are applying.*

Michael D. Griffin
Biographical Information

Michael Griffin is Space Department Head of Johns Hopkins University Applied Physics Laboratory (APL). Prior to joining APL he served in numerous executive positions with industry, including President and Chief Operating Officer of In-Q-Tel, Chief Executive Officer of Magellan Systems, General Manager of Orbital Science Corporation's Space Systems Group, and as Orbital's Executive Vice President and Chief Technical Officer.

Mike has previously served as both the Chief Engineer and the Associate Administrator for Exploration at NASA, and as the Deputy for Technology of the Strategic Defense Initiative Organization (SDIO). Prior to joining SDIO in an executive capacity, he played a key role in conceiving and directing several "first of a kind" space tests in support of strategic defense research, development, and flight testing. These included the first space-to-space intercept of a ballistic missile in powered flight, the first broad-spectrum, space-borne reconnaissance of targets and decoys in midcourse flight, and the first space-to-ground reconnaissance of ballistic missiles during the boost phase. He also played a leading role in numerous other space missions while employed at the Johns Hopkins Applied Physics Laboratory, the Jet Propulsion Laboratory, and Computer Science Corporation.

Mike has served as an adjunct professor at the University of Maryland, Johns Hopkins University, and George Washington University, offering courses in spacecraft design, applied mathematics, guidance and navigation, compressible flow, computational fluid dynamics, spacecraft attitude control, astrodynamics, and introductory to aerospace engineering. He is the lead author of over two-dozen technical papers, as well as the textbook *Space Vehicle Design*, and is a Registered Professional Engineer in Maryland and California.

Mike is the recipient of numerous honors and awards, including the NASA Exceptional Achievement Medal, the American Institute of Aeronautics and Astronautics Space Systems Medal, and the Department of Defense Distinguished Public Service Medal, the highest award that can be conferred on a non-government employee. He is a Fellow of the AIAA and of the American Astronautical Society, a member of the International Academy of Astronautics, and a Distinguished Alumnus of the University of Maryland's Clark School of Engineering.

Mike obtained his B.A. in Physics from the Johns Hopkins University, which he attended as the winner of a Maryland Senatorial Scholarship. He holds Master's degrees in Aerospace Science from Catholic University, Electrical Engineering from the University of Southern California, Applied Physics from Johns Hopkins, Civil Engineering from George Washington University, and Business Administration from Loyola College of Maryland. He received his Ph.D. in Aerospace Engineering from the University of Maryland.

Mike was born in 1949 in Aberdeen, Maryland. His hobbies include golf, flying, amateur radio, skiing, and scuba diving. He is a Certified Flight Instructor with instrument and multiengine ratings.

Getting to Know the Movers and Shakers

If you want to be a "mover and shaker," you need to know what they do and hang with them. Ross Macpherson wrote a good article that appeared in the April 11, 2005, issue of *JobSeekerWeekly* on learning how to get to know about and meeting "movers and shakers" in your industry. I say, *if you wanna be it, you gotta do it.*

Macpherson wrote, "The movers and shakers are those who stand at the pinnacle of the industry, who define where the industry is going, who understand the industry like no others, and who are tied in to everything that the industry is doing.

"Knowing the movers and shakers can do wonders for your networking and your career. If you are in their industry, or if you want to be, these are the people you need to know. The question is: How do you meet them?"

Macpherson wrote further, "Here are five of the best methods I know:

1. Read their articles

2. Become a member of professional associations

3. Attend conferences and introduce yourself to them

4. Communicate online with newsgroups, usenets, e-lists, or bulletin boards

5. Work on the right projects."[11]

---

[11] Ross Macpherson is the president of Career Quest, a certified professional resume writer and professional interview coach with over 12 years experience in career development and training. As an expert in "career marketing," Ross has helped thousands of professionals at all levels stand out from their competition and accelerate their career success through powerful resumes, job search techniques, and interviewing strategies.

Chapter 10 After Sending Your Resume

Waiting for the Call After You Send In Your Resume

I was wondering if you knew, typically, how long it takes for a well-known company to get back to you on your application for a job with about 100 applicants. I already submitted mine, but how can I make mine stand out in the future? Any help you can give me would be appreciated.

It varies anywhere from days to months. There is no set pattern. It depends on the following factors:

1. How closely your resume fits the position specifications
2. How badly they need to fill that position
3. How efficient the people in HR are in routing your resume and following up on it
4. How badly the hiring manager is pushing HR to fill the position
5. How many people applied for the position
6. I'm sure there are other factors

With all of these factors in play, nobody can accurately predict as to how long it takes a company, no matter how well known they are, to contact you for an interview. This is why it is important for you to get proactive and facilitate the process by adding your factor into the mix. Your factor is "following up" with the company.

After a week to 10 days, you should call the hiring manager or HR person in charge of that hire to let them know who you are, when you had submitted your resume, and ask them if they had seen it yet. You need to contact them continuously by phone, written correspondence (email and snail mail), and in person (if possible) to let them know how interested you are in the job. Be persistent but not pesky. Show them you're interested but not hard up. Keep on top of them. As a hiring manager, it always impresses me if a person continues to show interest in the position vacancy. So, don't overlook following up on the job. Go after it with a vengeance.

Here is a list showing you how you can make yourself stand out from all of your competitors (remember about discriminating yourself?) with the following:

1. Your resume
    a. Bullets that "pack a punch"
    b. Letter-perfect writing
    c. Type, bolding, font, paper
2. Your cover letter
    a. What to cover
    b. Your presentation
3. Your job searching strategies and tactics
4. Your follow up
5. Your interview
6. Your negotiations ability
7. Your job performance

Thanks for your reply. I actually attempted to call today, but they said they do not accept phone calls about applications and they will contact you if they want you. I was a little shocked about the whole thing. I want to follow up, but I really do not know how to go about it other than calling. It is for the San Diego Padres and they make it very difficult to contact the HR department and even more so the Management. Do you have any tips? ☺

That's how companies act whenever there is more supply than demand. They get really finicky and picky. They act like snobs. *The question is this:* Do you really want to work for a company who treats its recruits like dirt?

When you get into any company like that, don't forget how you were treated and do the opposite with anyone who calls. Treat them like human beings, respect them, show interest in them, give them the time of the day, etc. That's how you change a lousy company...one person at a time. Let that first person start with you.

Unfortunately, once people break in, they start falling into the groove; they start mirroring the corporate culture; and then, they start giving people who call in that same old mantra, i.e., Don't call us; we'll call you.

I write about incompetent HR departments in my book titled *What Hue is Your Bungee Cord?* Incompetent HR departments are what cause most of the hiring problems we have today.

The best way to break into any company is to have someone on the inside working to get you in. This is why networking is one of the most important tools and strategies for seeking a good job. If it wasn't for networking, I wouldn't have gotten most of my jobs. I wouldn't have been on the consulting gig I was on from January—March 2005 if it wasn't for networking. So, take maximum advantage of networking.

> *The best way to break into any company is to have someone on the inside working to get you in. This is why networking is one of the most important tools and strategies for seeking a good job.*

Seeking Resume Submittal Status

I sent my resume/cover letter to three firms and wasn't sure what is a normal time to hear a response. I assume that most firms go through their mail/emails within a few days, so I wasn't sure if that means they should call within about four to five days if they're interested. I will call when it hits a week though.

Yes, for a resume submission, a week to 10 days elapse time before calling would be about right. That way, if they haven't yet seen it, they would search for it. Usually, when you show such interest, they are more apt to be on the lookout for your resume because 99 percent of those who send in resumes usually don't ever bother to call and check to see if they had received it. You're doing the right thing!

Posting Resumes Online and Scam Companies

I suppose my question is this: Is it wise to post a resume online? Primerica and various other scam companies have also contacted me to attend their "group interviews." I thought I was a potential asset to a company, but now I feel silly and naive. Do you have a list of bad company red flags?

If you do not have a job and are looking for a job, I think it is okay to post your resume on reputable job websites such as monster.com, careerbuilder.com, flipdog.com, net-temps.com, dice.com, and hotjobs.com. However, if you already have a job but seek a better job, it could be risky to post your resume on any website, particularly if your current company could have access to your resume as well as to any others. The better way to go would be to use a recruiter or headhunter. However, only use recruiters/headhunters that you do not have to pay them any money.

I had a call once from Primerica who set up an interview with me. I did not feel good about that interview. After researching a bit on that company, I concluded that I would be wasting my time interviewing with them. Hence, I called them and canceled my interview.

Generally speaking, you should be wary of any company that displays any one or combination of the following characteristics:

- They charge you money for being involved with them in any way
- They want you to work strictly on commission
- They do not have a recognized, good name
- They meet in rundown facilities
- They give you a pitch that sounds too good to be true
- They won't give you any information on their company such as annual reports, 10K reports, annual revenues, number of employees, and list of employees you can call and talk with to ask them about the company
- You find news articles about their shady practices
- You feel uncomfortable around their people, facilities, and environment
- They want to pay you under the table
- They will not provide you any medical or other benefits
- They are in financial difficulties
- They have many lawsuits against them
- People you meet that have either worked there or know the company well continuously badmouth the company
- There are others that I can list here, but I will stop for now

> *You should only work for reputable, up-and-up companies and organizations.*

I hope this list helps. **Bottom Line**—*You should work only for reputable, up-and-up companies and organizations.*

Timing of Sending Out Resumes

How long before you graduate should you start sending out your resumes for possible job interviews?

You should *start sending out your resumes at least four months before you graduate.* In other words, if you will graduate in June, you should start at the beginning of the semester (i.e., January) to send out your resumes. Most companies understand that you will be graduating in the May-June timeframe. So, even though they may give you an offer in February or March, they understand that they will need to wait until June before they can bring you on board.

Some students make the big mistake of starting to send out their resume after they graduate. Others make an even bigger mistake by taking a month or more of vacation after they graduate and before they start their job search. It is not so bad in times when jobs are plentiful. However, in lean times, when unemployment is high, you cannot get started on your job search soon enough. In good times, you can find a good job in two to four months. However, in bad times, it could take you six months to a year to capture a good job.

> *"...start sending out your resume at least four months before you graduate."*

Timing of Sending Resume and Moving

If you are planning to move out of state after graduation, when should you send out your resumes? Are company's tentative to hiring someone who is not currently living close to the job even if they are planning to move to the area before the position is suppose to be filled?

There is no better time to start sending out your resume than the present. Make it very clear in your cover letter that you are planning on moving to the job location at such-and-such a time upon graduation. If you are good and represent just what the company is seeking, they will hire you no matter what.

If the company is a good one, they will even move you to the job area. If they are not that good, they will welcome your move to the area because they won't need to move you. Knowing that you would be moving to the area where the company is located could even be an incentive for them, in some cases, to pursue you.

If you're graduating in June, start your job search right now. It takes a few months to get a good job.

Chapter 11 Principles and Concepts to Remember

As we arrive at the end of this book, I list here some of the important principles and concepts for you to remember and continually apply throughout your career after you leave the classroom and enter the "real world." Here they are as follows:

Preparation

- Follow your passion.
- Seek jobs to which you can effectively apply your natural talents and that you thoroughly enjoy. *There is nothing better than to get paid for having fun.*
- Plan your career and then work your plan.
- You get what you expect. So, expect the best and get it.

Building Effective Resumes and Cover Letters

- The resume and cover letter are marketing/sales documents. Period!
- The only purpose of the resume and cover letter is to garner an interview.
- Keep your resume continuously updated throughout your career.
- Build resume bullets with "hooks" that "grab" the readers' attention, pack a "punch," and "wow!" them.
- Good resume bullets should be significant, detailed, factual, objective, quantitative, measurable, and "beefy."
- Good resume bullets should have both a feature and a benefit to them.

- Good resume bullets cover significant achievements, commendable accomplishments, superior performance, and outstanding results.

- Do not build resume bullets that mainly cover job descriptions, duties, and responsibilities.

A Final Word

Success is where preparation intersects opportunity. So, be prepared and do not "look a gift horse in the mouth." When the time is right, strike! To the victor go the spoils. Do not sit and watch the world pass you by. Strike first and make things happen.

Be a mover and a shaker. Be one who makes a difference and who adds value. Lead, follow, or get out of the way. If you will adhere to these principles, you will be a great success in your career and in life.

Success is 5 percent inspiration and 95 percent perspiration. Success is a journey, not a destination. Whatever the mind can conceive and sincerely believe can be achieved. Good luck!

Appendix   *Testimonials of Past Career Development Students*

These following statements are testimonials received from past students in my Career Development course:

- I want to let you know that I really loved this class, and I learned lots of new tricks. Thank you for teaching me how to make a good bullet. Thanks too that I may be getting a job by the end of this month. Thank you again.

- Great, thanks. Before I was one of those 99 percent who didn't call them. If they didn't call, I just assumed it wasn't good enough, and they were not interested. Because of you, I have "beefed" up my resume and encountered new experiences that make me feel more confident in sending out my resume and want to call. ☺ This class has really helped me a lot. I gained a better perspective on what employers look for in interview/resumes/cover letters/etc. It is great because I feel as though I have an advantage over the many students who get into the "real world" without this knowledge.

- Dear Professor Uda, Thank you so much on the advice you gave me and also for the timeliness of your reply. I just wanted you to know that the resume I created was created due to our class assignment and also for all the information you provided in class as they obviously helped me in getting this response. Enjoy the rest of your Spring Break and I will see you in class on Monday.

- This course proved to be extremely valuable to me though I am not beginning my initial career trek at this point in my life. The value was derived from the direct, sensible, and wise topical material and energetic teaching style that make up this course. The material is quality, and intrinsically enables one to gauge a comprehensive view of life in the "real world." Your instructional method consisting of sincerity, humor, and sharing personal SAR stories empirically pegged "real world" circumstances, unlike so many other courses. Presented as such in your expert and spirited way helped augment the education factor to the nth degree. You really care and it shows. That makes a big difference to students.

The presentation and flow (chapters and slides) of the material are excellent. The ambiance created in the classroom was one of optimism…the antithesis, intimidation, never materialized. The speakers were an added bonus and provided very insightful information. *There are not many more valuable writing assignments at the college level than creating and writing a personal resume and having an expert provide feedback on how it can be improved.* This course has no diminishing returns. In fact it is the opposite. The real value will be realized in the future by the many that follow and employ its tactile acumen.

- WOW! This is great information…something I have been pulling my hair out over. Bullets that pack a punch! Thanks. It is very helpful information. Please let us know when your book will be on the market.

- I wanted to also thank you for everything that you have taught me in this course. My cover letter and resume look 10 times better than before. I went into this course with little confidence in my resume and cover letter. I definitely see the value in having "bullets that pack a punch" and how they can definitely differentiate my resume from those of other candidates. Thanks for everything. I enjoyed your class.

- Before I took this class, I knew nothing about networking and selling myself. Now, I am gaining the confidence I need to approach people and start a conversation. I also have learned how to package myself by using tools such as a good resume and cover letter with "hooks" and having a strong network and the right attitude.

- This course can help every business student. There is a lot of information that you get out of this course that you won't get on your own. I think each student should learn how to do a resume that has bullets that pack a punch and put together a career portfolio. This was a very good course.

- My resume writing skills improved giving me greater confidence when trying to get an interview. This class is great, and I would recommend this course to every business student.

- Dear Professor Uda: I just wanted to send you a quick note to thank you for all of the lessons you taught me within your class. I learned a lot, which has helped me in implementing a successful job search. I am currently interviewing with many companies, and I believe that it was your help with my resume that got my foot in the door. Also, I am definitely using my SAR stories. I am interviewing with a company on Wednesday that requires five "pre-packaged stories" (i.e., SAR stories) for my next interview. Once again, thank you for all of your help, and I will keep you posted!

About the Author

Robert T. "Bob" Uda was born and raised in Hawaii for 20 years. He is the third of seven children of Masao and Irene Kuualoha Uda (both deceased). In the 40 years since leaving Hawaii, he has lived in Oklahoma, Ohio, Florida, Connecticut, and California with short stints in Utah, Alabama, Massachusetts, Texas, and Washington. He has traveled in 46 of our 50 states as well as in Canada and Mexico.

Bob earned BS degrees in aerospace engineering from the University of Oklahoma and in general business from Regents College of the University of the State of New York (now called Excelsior College). He further earned an MS degree in astronautics from the Air Force Institute of Technology and an MBA degree from the University of La Verne located in La Verne, California. Furthermore, he received a diploma in The Executive Program in Management from the UCLA Graduate School of Management.

Bob currently serves as professor of systems acquisition management at the Defense Acquisition University (DAU) where he teaches program management. He serves as a member of the Board of Regents (BOR) of the Institute of Certified Professional Managers (ICPM). Furthermore, he serves as director and vice president of the International Technology Institute (ITI).

In the USAF, he served as officer career manager of the Space and Missile Systems Organization (SAMSO), now called Space and Missile Systems Center (SMC). He held over 2,000 career counseling sessions with Air Force officers in the SAMSO on assignments, education and training, career broadening, and other personnel matters.

Bob has over 30 publications including nine books. One of these books is titled *Career Quest for College Graduates: Developing a Successful Career by Leveraging Each of Your Jobs*. A second book is titled *Career Quest for College Students: Career Development for Those Who Plan to Have a Successful Career*. A third book is titled *What Hue is Your Bungee Cord? Job Searching Strategies for Those Over 40 Years of Age*.

He taught logistics management courses to graduate students as an adjunct faculty member of National University. As a career coach with Bob Uda and Associates, he taught undergraduate students in "Career Development" at California State University San Marcos. He also taught "Writing and Publishing" with the Cal State San Marcos Extended Studies Office.

He is a fellow in the British Interplanetary Society, associate fellow in the American Institute of Aeronautics and Astronautics, executive member of the Academy of Management, Certified Manager (CM) with the Institute of Certified Professional Managers, and a founding charter member of the Association of Proposal Management Professionals.

He is listed in 46 Who's Who publications including *Who's Who in the World, Who's Who in America, Who's Who in California,* and *Who's Who in Science and Engineering.*

Bob and his wife, the former Karen Elizabeth Rowland of Circleville, Ohio, sired two sons, a daughter, and four grandchildren. You can contact Bob Uda by emailing him at bobuda@adelphia.net.

Index

978-0-595-38344-3
0-595-38344-0